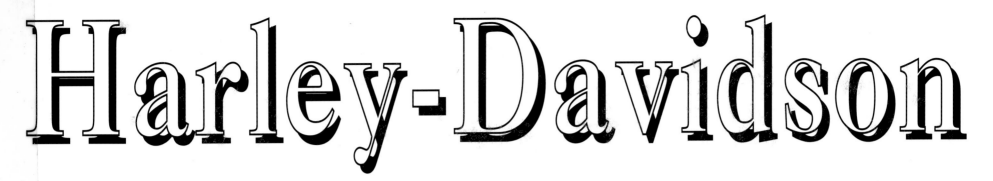

Harley-Davidson

A Worldwide Love Affair

Bright colours and low-riding style are typical of the modern custom Harley.

Harley-Davidson

A Worldwide Love Affair

Jim Glastonbury

 LONGMEADOW PRESS

Acknowledgements

We'd like to thank all those people who allowed us to photograph their beautiful Harleys, whether custom, historical or 'straight': Ronald Torbich, Chris Le Sauvage, Tommy Jansson, Ken Denison, Diana Villa, Tina Holtman, Ken Goldsbury, Dave Barr, Mark Bently, Pennie Lennon, John Low and Martin Gale. Invaluable help also came from those who restore and customize Harley-Davidsons for a living: Mallard Teal of Custom & Classic Restoration, Payne Avenue Body Shop, 860 Payne Avenue, St Paul, Minnesota 55101; Richard Taylor of Taylormade, PO Box 186, Tunbridge Wells, Kent TN1 2QW Great Britain; and Iain Cottrell, Harley 45 Specialist of Weymouth, Dorset, Great Britain. Harley 45 owners in Europe can contact the Harley-Davidson 45 Owners Club at 70B Parkview Rd, New Eltham, London SE9 3EQ. Apologies go to anyone we've omitted to mention.

The Harley poetry is reproduced by kind permission of its author, Martin Jack Rosenblum – all poems appear in his book *The Holy Ranger: Harley-Davidson Poems*.

Jim Glastonbury, Andrew Morland, England, February 1996

Harley-Davidson: A Worldwide Love Affair represents the private view of the author and is not an official Harley-Davidson publication.

RIGHT
'Harley Lady' at the Rat's Hole show.
Airbrushing allows delicate detailing (flowers are a popular subject) backed up, in this case, by a simple and elegant colour scheme.

Published by Longmeadow Press, 201 High Ridge Road, Stamford, CT 06904.

Cover and interior design by Annabel Trodd

ISBN 0-681-21554-2

First Longmeadow Press Edition.

Printed in China

Contents

This is what Main Street, Sturgis, looks like before two rows of motorcycles are parked down the middle of it.

Introduction

At the beginning of the century three young brothers and their next-door neighbour in Milwaukee decided to go into the motorcycle business. They had little idea of what they were starting. Arthur, Walter and William Davidson and their friend William Harley were unlikely tycoons. Like other young engineers at that time, they were enthusiasts, not entrepreneurs. Their idea was to build not a corporate empire but a practical motorcycle. Yet, from a shed in the back yard, an empire grew. In 1903 they made just three machines. Seventeen years after those first production bikes wobbled out onto the streets of Milwaukee, Harley-Davidson was the biggest motorcycle manufacturer in the world.

Though Harley-Davidson grew fast, it did not remain the biggest. Next to the Japanese giants of today, Harley-Davidson is a midget. Yet it survives, and the significant point is that, like such European bike makers as Ducati, Triumph and BMW, the impact of the Harley-Davidson name and image is out of all proportion to the size of the firm. Its fame has reached far beyond the limited circle of enthusiasts and is recognized by people who have never consciously seen a Harley-Davidson, let alone ridden one.

Ask any non-biker to name a few makes. They will inevitably mention one or two of the big Japanese corporations, plus Harley. For the general public, everything else belongs to a dim, mysterious world of speed, leather and loud exhausts. Is there any other consumer product (not a term the brothers would have liked to hear applied to a Harley) with such instant, world-wide recognition? Of course there are: Coca-Cola, Ford, McDonald's, for example. But all these are massive corporations with manufacturing plants all over the world, whereas Harleys have only ever been made in Milwaukee, Wisconsin, and York, Pennsylvania.

Internationally, the company is not big even among motorcycle manufacturers. Yet in the last few years it has become something of a cult, characterized by pens, notebooks, files, caps, buckles and badges, T-shirts and underwear, all bearing the Harley-Davidson logo, which for obvious reasons is now jealously guarded by the company. Few of the eager purchasers of these items have ever owned, ridden or even sat on a Harley.

Why has practically the whole world heard of Harley, and what is the attraction of the Harley image? The simple answer is that it's been around a long time. Having

LEFT

Exclusively solo: the big sprung saddle made a hard-tail rear end fine for the rider, but it wasn't much fun for the pillion. Sensibly, this bike accommodates parcels only.

RIGHT

Owner Mallard Teal restored this bike to stock spec. Apart from the modern tyres, this picture of suburban America could have been taken at any time in the past forty years.

BELOW

Mallard's more usual work involves customizing modern Harleys, so he couldn't resist the odd bit of extra chrome here and there. It sets off the deep red colour scheme.

BELOW

The suspension may have changed, but the 120mph (190kph) speedometer seemed to go on for ever. The tank mounting became so much an integral part of the big-twin look that it still has influence today.

started in 1903, Harley-Davidson is one of the oldest motorcycle manufacturers in existence. There were others active about the same time (the first Triumph took to the road a year earlier) but none has been in continuous production for so long.

Continuous production is the key. By motorcycle standards, H-D's corporate history has been remarkably stable. While other companies went into crisis, collapsed, revived, only to collapse again, Harley has kept going under more or less the same ownership. It experienced rough patches, of course. In the early thirties the four founders considered closing down permanently. After World War II the British and, later, the Japanese launched competitive onslaughts that came as a rude shock to a company accustomed to monopolizing the U.S. market. Harley-Davidson made three separate applications for trade tariffs against foreign imports. Ironically, they finally gained tariff protection under the Reagan administration, which was supposed to be devoted to the free market.

Another crisis occurred in 1969, when the industrial giant AMF took over Harley. Company presidents came and went faster than Italian prime ministers, assembly moved out of Milwaukee and, while production soared, quality nose-dived. Still, Harley-Davidson survived, and to this day the original family is still represented in the company. Willie G. Davidson, grandson of the original William, is currently head of styling. His son works for H-D too.

Continuity, though a powerful asset, is not the only reason for Harley's high profile. Equally important is the fact that it is the only American motorcycle in production, and has been for many years.

There was a time when American bike

OPPOSITE
A group from Chicago en route to Sturgis. Like many others, they stop off for sightseeing in South Dakota's Badlands.

RIGHT
Modern dresser style for a Minnesota-based Harley. Panniers, screen and extra lights front and rear are typical.

Two Shovelheads by the drag strip at Sturgis. You can see (and hear!) more straight-through pipes at Sturgis than anywhere else.

makers led the world in both production and technology. When Henry Ford produced the Model T, a car for the mass market, he put paid to many of them. The survivors were restricted to making bikes for enthusiasts. One by one, they fell by the wayside, leaving only Harley and Indian still in business.

Indian V-twins were faster than Harleys and, unlike Harley-Davidson, the company was not afraid of diversifying into fours and vertical twins, whatever it thought might sell. But Indian neglected its U.S. dealers even more than Harley did, and lacked Harley's continuity of leadership. It never really recovered after H-D leapfrogged ahead with the overhead-valve Knucklehead in 1936, though it did not finally collapse until 1953.

Only now, over forty years on, does Harley-Davidson appear to be facing homegrown competition once more. Encouraged by Harley's recent success, at least four attempts have been made to revive Indian since 1990. The Indian Motorcycle Kit Company promised fours in kit form in 1997. A fully built Chief V-twin was advertised for the millennium. In view of the legal wrangles and grandiose plans of previous would-be Indian makers, no one is thinking of placing firm orders just yet. More promising is the Confederate Gray Ghost, a performance V-twin using a 1525cc S & S engine and other input from Kosman Racing. Limited production was due to start in Spring 1996, with a projected price tag of $27,000.

Whatever the future may bring, Harley-Davidson has been the only bike maker to fly the Stars and Stripes for a very long time, and that helps to explain why the marque has such a following in the United States. Even among non-motorcyclists, its

reassuring continuity in an ever-changing world confirms its place in popular affection. There is a British parallel with the Morgan sports car, whose classic thirties look endears it to many people who know nothing about cars.

Harley's status as an American institution does not explain its popularity in other countries. The fascination of the rest of the world with the all-American Harley is a recent development. In Europe during the 1960s and 1970s, Harley-Davidson, if known at all, was regarded with something like contempt. Older people fondly remembered the WLAs that the U.S. army brought over in World War II, along with chewing gum and Hershey bars, but for motorcyclists the future lay with four-cylinder Hondas, two-stroke Kawasakis and, for a while, BSA/Triumph triples. Harley-Davidson's great lumbering dinosaurs seemed hopelessly outdated. So what changed?

The main reason why H-D is taken more seriously by the industry today stems from the great leap forward of 1984, the Evolution engine. It was quiet, reliable, civilized, and it didn't leak oil. As quality improved year after year, exports rose. Those who care about valve sizes and piston rings felt a new respect for the Harley. But so did a great many others.

Harley's universal popularity is part of a wider trend, the world-wide appeal of American popular culture as purveyed by films and TV, fast food and soft drinks. Even in Russia, cut off from the West for decades during the Cold War, some of the biggest queues ever seen in Moscow, the city of queues, formed outside the newly opened McDonald's. America may have lost some of its political prestige, but its popular culture still represents an ideal of

the good life to which millions aspire. Harley-Davidson is part of that. It summons up an image of the big, wide-open country, and the usual biking clichés about power, freedom and the open road belong more to Harley than any other bike.

Nostalgia is an important element in the popular dream. It is the Morgan syndrome again, the unchanging, classic design (however up-to-date it may be behind the façade) in an uncertain and unstable world. Harley has taken full advantage of this. It stopped trying to make its bikes look modern in the early 1970s. Since then, with increasing skill and astuteness, the company has opted for rolling nostalgia. The XLCR, which H-D called a café racer, was an exception; otherwise, bikes like the Heritage Springer and Softail have all traded skilfully on the fact that Harleys look old-fashioned. That is just what many people like about them. If an article looks old, we think, it must have character, something that makes it superior to bland, computer-designed, mass-produced competitors. Thousands of people may have the identical Harley-Davidson poster on their walls, yet the image still suggests non-conformity and individuality. There's an indefinable magic about that big V-twin that captures the imagination.

This bike is actually a late 1940s WL 45, restored in 1960s dresser style by Iain Cottrell, who specializes in 45 Harleys at his base in Weymouth, England.

The tank badge on this model J looks like those on the latest Harleys. The company used many different styles over the years but returned to the bold patterns of old once it realized the market value of nostalgia.

The Name Is Harley

standing there with the look
of invention in front of that
original shack new ideas took
hold which built a reputation
all the way into the American ideas

that govern individuality & style:
William S. Harley has lent his name

to the modern horsemen whose
apocalyptic ride strengthens
open trail visions that make

this photographic action take place
this sunrise in April as I take the
keys to my Harley machine then walk

the irregular stone path to
the garage contemplating in
poetic anticipation exactly
what will
be coming
within an
afternoon –
upon this
Iron Name.

Chapter One
Birth and Early Growth

Right from the start, the name was Harley-Davidson. Although there were three Davidsons to one Harley, and the Davidsons' father built the first 'factory' (actually a shed at the bottom of the garden), they all agreed that Bill Harley's name should come first. After all, he was the designer and draughtsman, the man who decided what should go where.

The son of English parents who had emigrated from Manchester, William Harley started out as an apprentice bicycle fitter in Milwaukee, Wisconsin. After a year or two he moved into the drawing office of the Barth Manufacturing Company. His friend and neighbour, Arthur Davidson, worked at Barth's too, as a patternmaker. The Davidsons had come over from Scotland in about 1871 and, by a fruitful quirk of fate, the two immigrant families ended up living next door to each other in Milwaukee.

A year younger than Bill Harley, Arthur Davidson shared his fascination with the petrol engine and possessed the practical skill to turn Harley's ideas into a working model. It was one of the great strengths of the partnership that the four founders possessed complementary talents. Arthur's elder brother Walter was a machinist, and when he came in to help build the early machines Arthur was able to exploit a

natural talent for selling, persuading cycle dealers to stock the new Harley-Davidson motorcycle. When they went into production, the eldest Davidson, William, joined them as works manager. His experience as an industrial foreman helped them through the first years of spectacular growth.

Besides their individual talents, they all shared a thoroughly practical engineering background and, equally important, an innate caution. They were always prepared to take time to make sure they had got everything right.

Bill and Arthur built their first engine in 1900, but five years passed before they moved into serious production. Bill Harley took several years off to study for an engineering degree. That kind of thoroughness, plus the variety of their skills, probably explains why Harley and the Davidsons succeeded where countless others failed. Many people were rushing into production with half-baked plans, bolting together parts bought from a catalogue, sometimes without fully understanding what they were doing. Naturally, they did not last long.

Arthur and William were more solid characters. They first considered small boat engines before, keen cyclists as they were,

they turned to motorcycles in the autumn of 1900. Their first 10ci (164cc) engine was just about able to propel a standard bicycle. Although the carburettor is said to have owed much to a tomato can, there was nothing particularly innovative about the engine, a typically crude De Dion derivation, and it lacked power. A 25ci (410cc) version soon followed, but that proved too much for the bicycle frame, so they decided they would have to design a frame from scratch. This was a significant decision, marking the move from what was merely a powered bicycle to a motorcycle proper.

The result, with its three horsepower, atmospheric inlet valve and whippy, leather, belt drive, was the first Harley-Davidson. It proved its reliablity in tests throughout 1903 and, when Bill Harley went off to college in the autumn, Arthur built two replica machines for paying customers. The price was $200, half payable on order, half on delivery, and both customers were thoroughly satisfied. Unlike most contemporary machines, the Harley-Davidson kept going.

Events speeded up a little the following year. Walter began to work full-time, the shed doubled in size, more orders came in. Still, they only built three bikes in 1904, five

Birth of a legend, the 1913 11F. In fact, Harley-Davidson was not a V-twin pioneer. Its first twin simply followed a current trend.

the year after. Capital was the main problem, but it was soon solved by a loan from a rich uncle. With the cash the partners bought land on what was to become Juneau Avenue and erected a two-storey factory, where they produced 49 motorcycles in 1906. (Harley-Davidson engines are still built there, though in rather larger numbers.) From then on the graph leapt upwards. Word of mouth, plus a prestigious contract to supply the police department, more than trebled sales in 1907. Next year was better, the year after better still, and in 1910 the Juneau Avenue plant, already enlarged, was making 3,000 bikes a year. Harley-Davidson had arrived.

The first full-production bike was called the Silent Gray Fellow, the name reflecting its quiet running and standard colour. It served the company well, and was to stay in production until 1918, but to keep up with the competition Harley-Davidson had to offer something more. That something was a V-twin.

Although, nowadays, it seems they should have done, and people often suppose they did, Harley-Davidson did not invent the V-twin. Theirs was not even one of the first. There were about 36 motorcycle manufacturers in the U.S.A. by 1908, and most of the larger outfits were building some sort of twin-cylinder engine, usually the narrow-angle V, with mechanical inlet valve but still relying on the old belt drive. The narrow angle (Harley's was 45 degrees) was far from ideal, as it produced unavoidable vibration, but there were many factors in its favour. Not only would it fit into existing frames without much trouble, it promised a large increase in power for little extra weight. Best of all, it demanded no major redesigning: you could simply double up

the existing single cylinders that everyone had started out with. Customers, confronted with North America's great distances, demanded more speed and power (one reason why American motorcycles grew bigger more quickly than European machines). In the circumstances, the V-twin was the obvious answer.

Harley's first twin of 1908 was something of a false start. With its atmospheric inlet valve (as on the old single), it was just not powerful enough. Another four years passed before H-D's definitive twin arrived. By then it was bigger, the classic 61ci (1000cc) size that the company was to stick with for decades. It had a mechanical inlet valve, allowing higher engine speed and thus more power, and it had a clutch and chain drive. The latter was a genuine H-D innovation. Bill Harley designed a proper multi-plate clutch that was far in advance of the fragile devices fitted by rivals. Another improvement was the 'Ful-Floteing' saddle, with a 14-inch coil spring inside the seat tube, while rivals were still making do with the old bicycle saddle. Harley-Davidson was becoming one of the leading makers. In 1913 they sold almost 13,000 bikes.

They were far from being the biggest. In that same year, Indian produced over 31,000, nearly half the national total, outselling every other company by a huge margin. That lead was soon to be reduced, as Harley-Davidson caught up and even surpassed the former market leader.

These developments arose largely from the circumstances of the world war, in which the United States became involved in 1917. Thanks to Arthur Davidson's hard work, Harley-Davidson had a wide dealer network, but there were still many places

where Indian controlled the franchise. Whether from patriotism or the profit motive, Indian turned over most of its wartime production to the army, starving its dealers of bikes. H-D also supplied the army, but on a far smaller scale, and the company was quick to recruit disgruntled Indian dealers and keep them well supplied with their own product. In these events lay the roots of the Indian v. Harley-Davidson feud that was to last until the final demise of the Iron Chief over thirty years later.

Like their rivals, Harley-Davidson did well out of World War I. The faithful old single was dropped at the end of the war, but the J-model twin now had more power, better lubrication and improved front forks. These were golden years for H-D racing, while the war had also provided the

opportunity to enter the export market for the first time. In 1920 a record 28,000 bikes were built at Juneau Avenue.

In fifteen years Harley-Davidson had gone from backstreet workshop to market leader. It was riding the crest of a wave. But the wave was about to break.

BELOW
The 61ci (1000cc) V of 1923 was still a distant development of the first single. The overhead-inlet/side-exhaust valve layout was about to be superseded by all side-valve operation.

FAR LEFT
The model J showing the overhead tappet and inlet system with side exhaust.

LEFT
Harleys of the 1920s weren't very radical, but there were still plenty of patents listed on the battery box.

Chapter Two
Victory Achieved — Eventually

Bill Harley and the Davidsons certainly came out of World War I well, so well that they seem to have been overcome by euphoria. They abandoned their native caution and embarked on some risky ventures, all financed by loans. The Juneau Avenue site expanded to 56,000 square metres (600,000 sq ft). With 2,400 workers and the capacity to turn out 35,000 bikes a year, it was the largest motorcycle factory in the world. An investment of half a million dollars in machine tools underlined the founders' confidence in the future, as yet unclouded by the Model T Ford. They had new models too, the European-influenced Sport Twin, new singles and side-valve V-twins.

Unfortunately, the future turned out to be less rosy than expected. After the boom came the postwar slump: the record production of 1920 halved to little more than 10,000 in the following year, and the recovery that followed was slow, painful and uneven. The main problem was Henry Ford. By the mid-twenties, his basic Model T was far cheaper than a big Harley with sidecar. Who was going to buy the H-D combination when he could have four wheels and protection from the weather while paying much less? The Model T and other inexpensive, mass-produced cars

that followed transformed the motorcycling industry. With economy no longer on its side, the motorcyle changed from a utility item to a luxury. A growing band of enthusiasts were still willing to pay for it, but the trouble with luxury articles is that, when times get hard, they are the first things that customers stop buying.

It was still possible to make a profit in the motorcycle business if you had the right products. Unfortunately, Harley-Davidson often did not. It wasn't that the founders had grown complacent, far from it. The Model W Sport Twin, announced to a startled world in 1919, was a radical innovation, a mild-mannered flat twin with up-to-the-minute multiplate clutch, fully enclosed chain, optional electric lights and coil ignition. The hope was that this six-horsepower 600cc machine, with its easy starting and low vibration, would attract a new type of rider. But it was also distinctly slow: 80kph (50mph) was the most that could be squeezed out of it. It was no great hit with a motorcycling public by now entrenched in their affection for the noisy, powerful V-twin. The Sport Twin's failure must have cut deep. Never again would Harley-Davidson try to sell the public anything but a single or a V-twin.

Every new bike, if not a flop like the

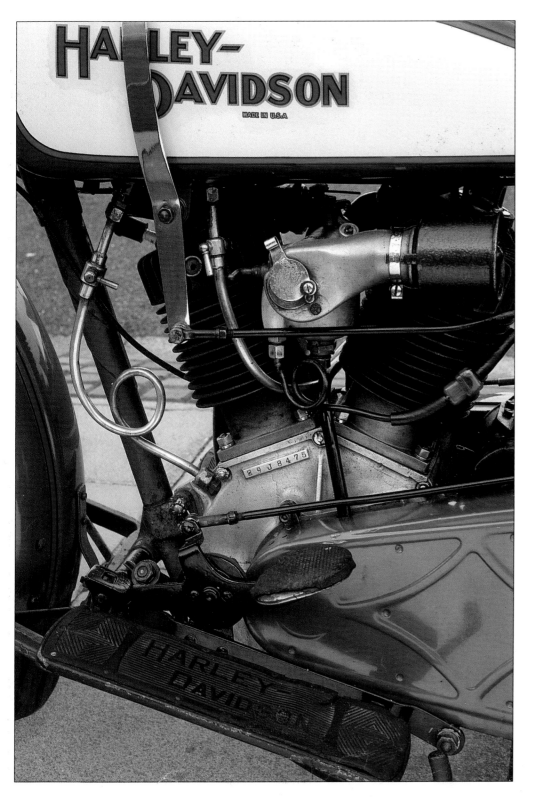

OPPOSITE
The 1929 J was one of the last ioe (inlet-over-exhaust) twins. The exposed valve gear shows its age, but some people considered the side-valve V series that followed was inferior.

LEFT
The other side of the 1929 J. Note the coils in the oil and fuel lines, which prevented vibration fractures, and the hand gear-change linkage. Harley persevered with hand changes years after most other makers had abandoned them.

ABOVE
The standard Harley tank-mounted speedometer read up to 195kph (120mph), which was even more fanciful on WLAs like this than on other Harleys. The WLA's speedo and its housing were identical with those of civilian bikes. Purists will note that the ignition switch on this wartime bike should be the same shade of khaki as the rest.

Sport Twin, had its own teething troubles. The 45 V-twin was simply too slow; the VL side-valve vibrated; the 61E Knucklehead was fast but leaked oil; the postwar Panhead's hydraulic tappets gave trouble, and so on. It began to look as if the founders, who had spent so long perfecting their first single, were now less concerned with producing reliable, trouble-free machines than with beating Indian.

At least they were successful in that objective. In 1923 they outsold their great rival by about 50 per cent. But the rivalry was becoming almost an obsession. When the company's publicity manager, Hap Scherer, was sacked on the spot for co-operating with an industry survey, paranoia seemed to be creeping in. (Ironically, the survey gave H-D a clean bill of health, commending its efficiency and widespread dealer network.) There were stories of other ruthless business practices, such as obtaining lucrative police contracts by selling bikes at cost and destroying the rival machines surrendered in part exchange. This kind of behaviour did nothing to endear Harley-Davidson to the trade in general or to Indian in particular.

But the riders themselves were not disillusioned. The 61ci (1000cc) Model J was for many the definitive big twin in the

1920s. Here, surely, lies the origin of the Harley image as, above all, the manufacturer of simple, no-nonsense V-twins. Popular with policemen and (sidecar attached) with postal workers, as well as ordinary riders, the J kept Harley going all through the uncertain twenties. Its only market weakness was that some rivals had more power, and H-D answered that in 1922 with the superpowered Twin, a bigger, 74ci (1200cc) version of the J. It was originally designed as a sidecar tug, but solo riders enthusiastically welcomed its extra power.

The side-valve VL had a less happy reception. Although the company claimed a 15 per cent increase in power over the J, the new bike was much heavier. It vibrated horrendously at speed and the small flywheels destroyed its torquey feel. It suffered especially by contrast with some of the last Model Js, the legendary 'Two Cammers' (twin cam), with an alleged potential of 160kph (100mph), far beyond the capacity of the pudding-like VL. The latter's faults were eventually corrected, which involved the virtual rebuilding of the bike from scratch with new flywheels, crankcases and frame, and the VL went on to inherit the mantle of the well-loved J, but in its original form it made an inauspicious start to the 1930s.

Similar problems affected the 45, Harley's 'small' V-twin which first went on sale in 1929. It shared its frame with the 500cc single, superficially a sensible piece of rationalization which, however, had the unfortunate effect of lumbering the single with too heavy a chassis while it gave the V-twin nowhere to put its generator. They had to mount it vertically in the end, prompting satirical remarks about 'the first three-cylinder Harley' and leading to drive-

gear failure. Moreover, the 45 was slow, so slow that the factory rushed out a carburettor kit to boost performance. That was some help, but the 45 remained the sluggard of the range for the rest of its remarkably long life, especially compared with the contemporary Indian Sport Scout, not to mention the 150kph (90mph) Excelsior Super X. Its saving grace was its reliability. Powering the three-wheeled Servicar, and the wartime WL solo, it chugged relentlessly on, surviving in its Servicar guise until 1974, nearly half a century after its unpromising introduction!

The Servicar represents another aspect of the H-D story and really deserves a book of its own. Just when the motorcycle market seemed to be shrinking into a small band of enthusiasts, Harley discovered a different outlet altogether. With a motorcycle front end and two wheels at the rear, the Servicar proved a remarkably adaptable vehicle. More stable than a conventional sidecar outfit, it was used for years by garages to tow broken-down cars, by police, meter maids and mailmen. In economy, compactness and price, it was close to a motorcycle, and yet it served as a useful small delivery van. In that guise it remained entirely an American phenomenon. In Europe, the niche in the market was filled by numerous small four-wheel vans.

It may have been partly the image of the Servicar, as well as the modest performance of the side-valve V-twins, that gave Harley something of a reputation as an old man's machine: reliable (at least after the hasty rebuilds), a known quantity, but hardly exciting. Indians might not hold together so well, but they were a lot quicker. In the early thirties, all this was about to change. The transformation in

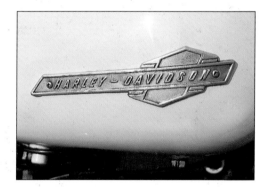

Harley's image was due entirely to one bike, the renowned Knucklehead.

The Knucklehead, whose less evocative, formal name was the 61E, was the founders' statement of faith in the future. After a healthy year in 1929, the Wall Street Crash and the subsequent Great Depression devastated the motorcycle industry. In 1933 Harley produced just 3,703 bikes, less than 20 per cent of the 1929 production. It was about this time that the founders, who were no longer young, talked seriously about giving up the business altogether.

Instead, they took the farsighted decision not only to stay in production but to invest scarce funds in a genuinely new and modern bike. It wasn't only that the Knucklehead had overhead valves. A dry sump and recirculating lubrication at last banished the antediluvian total-loss system. It had a four-speed (three gears were thought quite enough until then), constant-mesh transmission and a new frame. With its tapering tank and art deco badge (actually introduced in 1931, three years earlier), the Knucklehead looked good too. It was fast (150kph/90mph), revved harder and produced more power than any other Harley twin. The dealers liked it, and it sold.

Like all pre-war Harleys, it suffered some early traumas. The new dry-sump system delivered too little oil to some parts of the all-new top end and too much to others. As a result, the top end leaked oil. That did not worry those used to the messy total-loss system, but it marked the birth of another unfortunate Harley legend, which the company did not shake off until the 1980s. Some 1,900 Knuckleheads passed down the assembly line before a solution was found.

It was important that the solution *was* found, because the big side-valves, renamed the UH and ULH, adopted dry sumps in 1936. The 61ci V was dropped, and the 74ci was joined by the even larger 80ci (1300cc), designed primarily for sidecar work. With the 61ci Knucklehead filling the role of sportster (twenty years before the Sportster with a capital S), the slow-revving side-valves could concentrate on what they did best, propelling sidecars and riders over huge distances. They were none too quick about it, but they got there in the end.

LEFT
Joe Petrali's record-breaking 218kph (136mph) Knucklehead helped to boost Harley-Davidson's image, but Walter Davidson refused him a bonus, saying he hadn't gone fast enough!

ABOVE
A WLA equipped for the rigours of war, with rifle scabbard within easy reach, copious panniers and big-clearance mudguards. The WLA might not be everyone's idea of an off-road bike, but more often than not that was where it went.

Another war was looming, and this time it wasn't enough to paint the civilian models in olive drab and send them off to the front. The 45ci (750cc) D was transformed into the WLA (A standing for Army). It was detuned, insofar as that was necessary; larger cooling fins and oil-bath air filter helped it run cooler and cleaner. It had bigger wheels, with knobbly tyres, and a steel skid plate. Typical combat specification included a Thompson submachine-gun holster on the front forks, ammunition box, leather panniers, blackout lamps, windshield and leg guards. Some machines were fitted with what looked like a thick radio aerial at the front: its actual purpose was to cut through wire strung across the road, thus saving the rider from decapitation. With all this additional gear, the WLA could barely reach 80kph (50mph), but its reliability became legendary.

Never slow to capitalize on a propaganda opportunity, H-D exploited the WL's front-line performance to publicize the company's part in the war effort. Issues of *The Enthusiast*, Harley-Davidson's house magazine, carried picture-stories of brave G.I.s patrolling the war zone on WLs, through desert, mud and Asian jungles. There was nothing new in the Harley's role as the spearhead of combat. It is said that the first U.S. serviceman to cross the German border during World War I did so on a Harley sidecar outfit.

The WLAs were not H-D's only combat bikes. For the Canadians 20,000 WLCs (C for Canada) were turned out, with right-hand clutch, foot change, and the brake on the left. Other war machines were more radical. The Canadians were interested in a mini-tank powered by two 61ci (1000cc) Knucklehead engines, and there were

SHIP.WGT.-535LBS
O-LGTH-88INS
O-HT-59INS
O-WIDTH-37INS

LEFT

A massive air cleaner and all-over khaki were standard WLA spec. This one dates from 1942.

BELOW

All the military gear plus a fully equipped rider gave a gross weight of 400kg (885lb) and made life hard for the side-valve 45ci (737cc) V-twin engine, but its mild state of tune guaranteed reliability.

BELOW

In case the rider forgot: engine and transmission used the same grade of oil, but different grades were needed for the extreme variations of climate in which a WLA might have to operate.

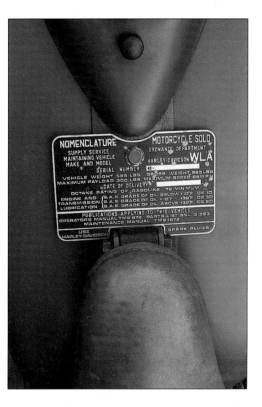

several forms of the flat twin XA, although it never shared the WL's success. The army wanted a shaft-drive machine suitable for the desert, and the XA was Harley's response. It looked suspiciously similar to the BMW flat twin. The company built a thousand of them in motorcycle form, but the end of the North African campaign made them redundant. There were also plans for an XA-powered mini-Jeep and a preliminary massive order for XA generator sets, which came to nothing.

The WLA came out of the war covered in glory. Not only was it utterly reliable, it introduced thousands of G.I.s to motorcycling in general and to Harley-Davidson in particular. When they came home, many wanted to keep riding.

The end of the 1940s marked the end of an era for Harley-Davidson in at least one sense. Arthur Davidson and his wife were killed in a car accident. His brother William had died before the war, Walter in 1942 and Bill Harley in 1943, but in practical terms the passing of the last of the four founders of the company meant little. It was business as usual, with a new generation of both Harleys and Davidsons taking over and a third generation, who would move into the boardroom in the 1960s, already on the horizon: Willie G., then a bespectacled youth with a sensible haircut, would join the styling department in 1963. Even after the public flotation of the company in 1965, the two families kept majority control, and there was no major change of direction until the American Machine and Foundry (AMF) takeover in 1969.

There is a case for arguing that the continuous family control did Harley-Davidson no good. The people running the company were there because of their family, not for any particular business ability. Continuity can also imply conservatism. The safest policy was one of no change, and since the V-twins had put the company where it was, and had made the families a lot of money, why risk

change? The experience of Indian provided a warning. In a last-ditch effort to survive, Indian produced a range of small singles and V-twins to confront the competition from Britain. They were mechanical disasters and, rather than saving Indian, they speeded its progress to the grave.

Harley-Davidson contemplated no such rash expedients, and for some years after 1945 their cautious policy seemed well justified. Thousands of G.I.s returning from the war were keen to buy a motorcycle, and consumers in general had money to spend. The war years, and the preceding economic depression, had bottled up demand. Now, the times were prosperous. Even the less well-off could afford a motorbike, if only a second-hand one. It was a seller's market. In 1948 Harley-Davidson recorded its best year to date, with over 30,000 bikes built and sold.

Better still, with the disappearance of Indian in 1953, Harley had the big-bike market all to itself, True, an increasing number of Nortons, BSAs and Triumphs (over 15,000 in 1947) were being imported, but these were little bikes. It could be said that that they performed a useful service in attracting new riders who in time would graduate to a 'real' bike – a Harley. (Some years later the British makers were to

comfort themselves with the same illusion when contemplating competition from Japan.) It was also said, with some truth, that the British bikes lacked the stamina of a Harley. Finally, the social climate of America in the 1950s, when intense patriotism was tinged with xenophobia, favoured native manufacturers. Whatever its other virtues, Harley-Davidson was American, a strong point in its favour.

The large band of Harley loyalists was as dependable as ever, and it was growing. The big V-twins kept selling, and changes were few. The first of any note was the 1947 Panhead. All the 'head' names, incidentally, were strictly unofficial and stemmed from the shape of the rocker covers, which variously reminded people of knuckles, saucepans or shovels. Some people called the Evolution the Blockhead, but that one, not surprisingly, never caught on.

The main advance in the Panhead was the change to alloy cylinder heads, to avoid the overheating that the iron heads of the Knucklehead had been prone to, with hydraulic tappets. The automobile industry had been using hydraulic tappets for some time. They promised more consistent valve clearances and timing, lower maintenance and quieter running. Unfortunately, the

Full-dress saddle, mudguards, duotone and chrome: it looks like a touring FL, but is it?

LEFT

A proud owner poses on his Panhead outfit, recently rescued from Bolivia. This particular bike was rumoured to have been part of the Presidential Guard.

RIGHT

A 1993 Electra Glide, built for performing a traditional task though the owner of this one obviously believes that accessories make a motorcycle!

Panhead complied with a long Harley tradition by failing to fulfil these promises, at least to begin with. The main problem was that the tappets were at the top of the engine but the oil pump was at the bottom. The labyrinthine oil-ways between the two caused surges in oil pressure, which naturally did nothing at all for the valve timing. The solution was to move the tappets to the base of the pushrods, but it took six years for Harley to make that obvious change, and the Panhead still leaked oil.

Like all the earlier big twins, the Panhead was steadily updated. It acquired hydraulic front forks in 1949, ending the era of the old springers designed by Bill Harley which had been a Harley trademark since 1908. (In another forty years they were to return in stylized, computer-designed form.)

For the first time, Harley gave this machine a trade name, the Hydra-Glide. It gained an extra ten horsepower in 1950 and a foot gear change in 1952, although the hand change remained an option for traditionalists. In 1958 it became the Duo Glide, with swinging-arm rear suspension, a feature that the traditionalists had to put up with, like it or not.

The last and biggest transformation of the old Panhead was the famous Electra Glide of 1965. Electric start and 12-volt electrics showed that Harley-Davidson was not completely sunk in complacency. The massive starter motor and its accoutrements weighed a formidable 34kg (75lb), which as someone pointed out was not very much less than the weight of a whole Honda moped. Push-button starting did not appeal to some traditionalists, and

in wet weather shorting out was not unknown. Perhaps the biggest selling point was simply the evocative name. For many people the Electra Glide became the definitive big twin, embodying all that was good about a full-dresser Harley. It was the ultimate expression of the cruiser tradition of Harley-Davidson, and the name is still used for the top-of-the-range, fully equipped bikes. Adherents of the sportster or custom traditions of Harley ownership would never consider buying one, but for the tourers, perhaps the oldest and most significant of the three types of Harley owner, the Electra Glide is the only bike to have.

While the big twins were being developed into full-dress tourers, the Sportster range was getting under way. Its origins lay in the old 45, which remained in production after the war, chiefly for fleet buyers. Any private owner, especially the new generation, was unlikely to be attracted to this heavy and underpowered bike. Outclassed by Indian twenty years earlier, it had no hope of keeping up with the British singles and twins, which had smaller engines but were lighter, faster, a lot more nimble, and less expensive.

To combat the British, H-D was developing a new, 60-degree aluminium V-twin with twin carburettors called the KL. Meanwhile, the new Model K, which William H. Davidson described as a stopgap, was introduced in 1955. It certainly looked modern, with an up-to-the-minute chassis, hydraulic forks, swinging-arm rear suspension and foot change. All this might be a match for a Norton, but the V-twin was a 45ci (750cc) side-valve engine with a less than remarkable thirty horsepower. Exactly how closely it was related to the old 45 is a matter of

argument but, whatever its antecedents, it was not enough to frighten the opposition, even when extended to 55ci (900cc) in 1955.

The real breakthrough came two years later with the XL Sportster. This incorporated the up-to-date cycle parts of the K and added overhead valves, producing forty horsepower at 5,500rpm. At last Harley had an answer to the imports. It looked good, went well, and had a similar

effect on H-D's image as the Knucklehead twenty years before. All the same, this was not the bike to save the company. Throughout the 1960s the XL made up only about 25-30 per cent of total production. It was always far outnumbered by the big twins. Its most important contribution was to create a third Harley tradition. First there were the tourers with their big twins. Then, since the war, the customizers had been hard at work. Sportster owners were a new

breed, essentially performance-minded.

Fortunately, the XL proved particularly tuneable. The first official performance boost came with the high-compression, magneto-equipped XLCH (CH stood for 'Competition Hot'). Both XLs got higher-lift cams in 1959 and by 1969 power had been raised to 68bhp at 6,800rpm. Individual owners were 'stroking' the XL engine to produce even better performance. Although the Sportster acquired an electric start and

could be dressed up as a mini-Electra Glide, essentially it continued to represent the Harley sporting option. In the early 1960s it was one of the fastest things on the road. Eventually it was to be left behind in the horsepower race, but by that time H-D had realized that it couldn't compete with the Japanese for sheer speed, and sensibly did not attempt to do so.

Meanwhile, the company was sailing in dangerous waters. It was making as many

OPPOSITE

The 1950s-class dresser was a favourite for the FLH in all its forms. Whitewall tyres and white, streamlined panniers are period extras.

LEFT

Behind that impressive horn lies the Panhead, Harley's first major update of the Knucklehead. Its adoption of hydraulic tappets owed more to car than motorcycle practice.

motorcycles as ever (36,000 plus in 1966), but while sales remained about steady the size of the market was increasing by leaps and bounds. By the time the Electra Glide appeared, H-D's share had shrunk to a mere 6 per cent. Attempts to get into the small-bike market by buying into the Italian company Aermacchi met with only limited success. Harley-Davidson still had nothing between the Aermacchi 350cc single and the Sportster. Even the big twins were vulnerable, with Japanese fours threatening to poach the tourers' market. Simply put, Harley was in desperate need of new models but lacked the money to develop them. The time had come for Harley-Davidson to forsake its long-cherished independence and put itself up for offers.

There were two contestants. Bangor Punta was a company based on the manufacture of railway rolling stock. The AMF made industrial machinery. AMF won the battle, and has since incurred the hatred of diehard H-D loyalists but, looking back, it is difficult to see what alternative there was. Harley could not have survived on its own, and Bangor Punta had an unsavoury reputation as an assest stripper. It is unlikely that H-D would have long survived under that régime.

AMF was not an asset stripper and spent millions of dollars equipping its plant at York, Pennsylvania, to assemble Harleys. At first, it was even willing to invest in research and development of new models. The master plan was to boost production and, by making H-D a mass producer of motorcycles, take advantage of the expanding market to generate profits that would fund new models. AMF certainly succeeded in raising production, from 37,600 in 1971, to nearly 60,000 in 1972 and over 70,000 the following year. The

corollary was that quality plummeted. Dealers were forced back into the role of quality control and damage limitation, and the AMF Harleys acquired a bad name. Some bikers still refuse to recognize them as genuine Harleys. Management was poor. There was a lack of communication between the York plant and Milwaukee, now confined to making engines and gearboxes. Morale sank, and Japanese competition was as fierce as ever. As the motorcycle market flattened out, AMF was forced to acknowledge that Harley would not generate the hoped-for investment income in the forseeable future.

It wanted out.

In the absence of other offers, a management buy-out was the only solution. With a mixture of bank loans and employee investment, in 1981 Chairman Vaughn Beals and the Board, which still included a Davidson (Willie G.), persuaded AMF to sell Harley-Davidson for about $80 million. The last half million was allegedly settled by the toss of a coin. The deal, which included York, Milwaukee and of course the prized Harley-Davidson name, was actually quite a good one: the company had been valued at $300 million. It was greeted with general euphoria.

The directors symbolically rode back to Milwaukee, dealers painted out the AMF on their shop fronts, and everyone seemed overjoyed that, once more, 'the eagle soars alone'.

What they failed to realize was that the eagle was in imminent danger of a crash landing. Harley-Davidson was losing money, and needed to start earning it fast if only to pay the interest on loans. The motorcycle market was still flat, there was a big inventory of unsold bikes, productivity was low and quality remained a serious headache. A detailed analysis of how the company was turned around is given in

Peter Reid's *Well Made in America*, but basically a combination of ideas popularized by the big Japanese companies was responsible. Employee involvement harnessed the knowledge and experience of shop-floor workers. The Just-in-Time delivery service obviated expensive inventories, and every worker became a quality controller, responsible for quality at his or her stage of production.

The new methods brought instant improvement in quality and production. In fact, Harley was able to exploit a useful sideline teaching other American businesses what they had learned the hard way. But nothing would have made much difference in the absence of a successful product. Lack of money forced the abandonment of the ambitious NOVA programme hatched under AMF, which comprised a family of water-cooled engines of 500-1300cc. Much work had also been done under AMF on a comprehensive update of the old V-twin, named the Evolution, and this was to prove Harley's salvation.

Launched in 1983, the Evolution marked a real turning point. By Japanese standards it was still laughably underpowered, but that was no longer a vital issue. The Evolution engine was an evolutionary, rather than revolutionary, advance on the basic 45-degree push-rod V-twin. Reliability, low emissions and oil tightness were the main criteria, so great efforts were made to prevent overheating. Aluminium barrels replaced the iron ones and the air flow around the heads was much improved. Electronic ignition was by now standard, and there were closer tolerances all round. The Evo did not leak oil nor burn it. It produced 10 per cent more power than the Shovelhead (the last

LEFT
Electra Glide in black and white, over-engineered perhaps, but the electric start gave Harley a better chance of keeping its police business, at least for a while.

OPPOSITE
A Sportster XL1200 at Weymouth on the south coast of England. With the basic 883 becoming the entry-level Harley, the 1200 is the closest thing the factory now makes to a genuine sportster type.

manifestation of the old Panhead) and 15 per cent more torque. Best of all, it had no teething troubles. At long last, Harley had produced a bike that worked perfectly first time.

The role of the Evo in turning Harley's fortunes can hardly be overstated. Here was a Harley engine that provided Japanese convenience: quiet, or quietish, well-behaved and reliable. It looked like a traditional V-twin and made the right noises, though they were a little muted, but

it did not act like one. It was primarily responsible for creating a new breed of Harley riders, who were attracted by the image but were not weekend mechanics.

It is tempting to see the Evolution as a symbol of the new freedom of Harley-Davidson after its escape from the control of AMF, but it was really a product of the AMF era. The decision to proceed with it was made as early as 1976, several years before the management buyout, and work on it had continued ever since.

Part of the Evo's success was due of course to the 'retro' look; it appeared much older than it really was. The extension of this traditional feel to the rest of the motorcycle also explains Harley's success in the past ten years. The company had become aware of the importance of styling much earlier. The Super Glide of 1970 was an early sign, a bike whose styling, rather than its engine or some technical update, was the main selling point. It was basically a collection of existing parts, a big twin and

frame married to a Sportster front end; comparatively few parts of the bodywork were actually new. The Super Glide was a belated acknowledgement of what the customizers had been doing for years, not only because it was deliberately styled but also because it was built up from the Harley parts bin. It was an immediate success: 4,700 were sold in the first year of production.

From then on there was no stopping Willie G. and the styling department. They had cottoned on to the fact that new-looking models could be produced quite cheaply by swapping parts around and introducing some canny restyling. Drawing on Harley's rich history, they designed bikes that bikers could relate to and wanted to buy. Harley-Davidson was learning how to exploit its own past.

An exception to this trend was the XLCR Café Racer, an all-black, sporty-looking bike with bikini fairing and a contemporary, 1970s profile. It was not a great success and lasted only a couple of years. It taught a simple lesson: to sell, a Harley had to look like a Harley. Nothing else was 'authentic'. The company showed it had learned the lesson in 1978 with the FXS Low Rider. While not a faithful copy of the real custom low riders, it did have a very low seat, two-into-one exhaust, fatbob tank and old-style tank badge. Available with 1200 or 1300cc engine, it was another hit, selling nearly 10,000 in the first year.

Since the 1980s a bewildering array of models has appeared, all based on one family of engines but with their own special appearance. The names can become confusing: Tour Glide, Dyna Glide, FLHTCU I Electra Glide, Ultra Classic (top of the range in 1966), and so on. And who but Harley could get away with calling a

motorcycle 'Fatboy'? To list every variation would be tedious, but the following represent significant milestones.

The Sturgis (1980), named after the Black Hills Motor Classic, was the bike that introduced toothed rubber belt drive to Harley-Davidson. The belt was cleaner, quieter and smoother than a chain, and was soon fitted to all the big twins. The Sturgis was basically the FXS Lowrider, with the 80ci (1300cc) Shovelhead twin plus the new belt drive.

The XR1000 (1983) was something more than a restyle. Capitalizing on the XR750's flat-track success, the 1000 was a detuned road version. New barrels and pistons on the Sportster bottom end gave 998cc capacity producing 70bhp at 5,600rpm. *Cycle World* recorded 0 to 96kph (60mph) in 4.9 seconds and a top speed of 112mph.

The Sportster 883 (1985) was the bike that lured many riders back from Japanese machines. It was the old Sportster revitalized by a new, smaller Evo engine, returning to the classic 55ci (883cc) size. The company was so confident of its resale value that it guaranteed repayment of the retail price ($3,995) if traded in for a larger machine.

The Softail (1987) catered to those riders who wanted a bike that looked old but provided modern comfort and convenience. The rear shocks were hidden horizontally between gearbox and rear wheel, giving the frame a hard-tail look but without the hard ride.

The Springer Softail (1989) was the ultimate retro, using a new version of the old springer front fork which Harley-Davidson said had been computer-designed. With the necessarily skinny front wheel, performance was inferior to

hydraulic forks, but it looked the part, the softail frame suggesting a 1920s design.

Fatboy (1990) exemplified the low, solid, indeed 'fat' look, with disc wheels, low-slung softail frame and silver colour scheme. Shotgun-style exhaust (short, twinned pipes) and tank-mounted speedometer completed the picture.

The Dyna Wide Glide (1993) was another chopper lookalike, with high-rise bars (not too high, though, as some states had introduced legal restrictions on

handlebar height), bobbed rear mudguard and widely spaced forks for an imposing front-end look. The 'Dyna' element in the name implied a rubber-mounted engine.

Some people might say – have said, in fact – that this constant restyling is no substitute for engineering progress, and that it panders to riders more concerned with the way a bike looks than the way it performs. But, whatever purists may say about this nostalgia-based mix 'n' match policy, it has made Harley-Davidson what it is today – profitable.

ABOVE
Pure nostalgia is the motif of this Heritage Softail. Harley's retro bikes lend themselves so well to the old-world look that some owners like to go the whole hog.

RIGHT
Ronald Torbich with his Springer Softail and friends at Daytona Beach. The Springer's skinny front end makes a striking contrast with that of a Fatboy.

OPPOSITE
A bronzed Diana Villa enjoys Torbich's Springer at a traditional location. The Springer is Harley's most blatant piece of retro engineering yet.

FAR LEFT
This bike is more or less standard body-wise, with the fatbob tank and valanced rear mudguard as they left the factory.

LEFT
Mallard Teal does his own paintwork. It is interesting that painters are not afraid to indulge their own interpretation of the Harley-Davidson logo.

OPPOSITE
A mildly customized 1977 FXE, owned by Mallard Teal. The new paintwork and high bars do not obscure the long, low profile that made the FX Super Glide famous.

A 1992 Fatboy at the Goodwood racing circuit in southern England. Since some people derided Harleys as heavy, slow and 'fat', the company decided to call their bluff.

Harley and the Art of Motorcycle Magnificence

do not give me any
of that Zen & some

art of motorcycle
maintenance stuff:

just ride your
bike & if it is

not a Harley-Davidson
then maybe you should

just affix it to where
the sun don't rise any

place except through
those rustholes upon

foreign designs stuck
out on American roads.

Chapter Four
Custom Harleys: Birth and Stagnation

Customizing has been part of motorcycling almost since the beginning, and Harley-Davidson has always been involved. In fact, customizing or personalizing the bike is associated more with Harley owners than those of any other make. It seems to go with the territory. The first thing a typical Harley rider does to his or her new bike is to change it in some way, to make it personal to them, even if only by adding a Live to Ride points cover.

As a result, there are few stock Harleys around. Many may be customized in the same way, but very few appear exactly as they did when they left the factory. For the really serious customizers, Harley-Davidson is far and away the most favoured, at least in the United States. You may see the odd customized Triumph or BSA at Daytona Beach, but not many. It's not hard to see why. The massive V-twin engine is a visual statement in itself, a striking centrepiece that makes any custom Harley a real eyeful. And that – making the bike a visual attraction – is what it's all about. Other motives may be at work – to make the bike lighter, faster or more nimble – but looks are what customizers are chiefly concerned with.

It wasn't always like that. In the very early days, customizing often consisted of making parts yourself just to keep the bike going! It was not until the late 1920s that a definite 'look' developed, with Harley and Indian both involved. Since Henry Ford had undermined the motorcycle as basic transport, the big V-twins had become enthusiasts' bikes. What the enthusiasts liked most was touring, and their bikes reflected that. Fundamental changes to frame or engine were rare; accessories were the essence of it. The tourers' bikes sprouted all kinds of add-ons – screens, spotlights, panniers and big comfy saddles. This was the dresser style, a peculiarly American look designed for long rides out towards the horizon.

The dresser gradually became something of an institution. Touring clubs offered awards for the the best-turned-out bike and rider. In the custom Harley, or any other custom bike, changes may have been made for practical reasons, but the look they created became an object in itself. In the motorcycle clubs that grew up in the thirties and forties, members wore smart, twin-buttoned uniforms, identical peaked caps, riding breeches and boots. Penalties, though good-humoured ones, were levied on those who turned up without a tie. This military style was encouraged

LEFT
Another much-modified W, a WLC owned by John Low.

BELOW
Dresser-style spotlamps, massive saddle and panniers seem to be popular among WL owners, especially in Eastern Europe where for a long time the only Harleys available were leftovers from the war.

RIGHT
A chrome-bedecked view from John Low's WLC.

by Harley in particular. It presented the acceptable face of motorcycling. Riders were clean-cut, all-American sportsmen and women. Motorbikes represented a healthy, clean-living life style for middle America.

In later years, after the film *Easy Rider*, innumerable horror stories about Hell's Angels, and media portrayals of the biker as social outcast, made that image came to seem laughable. But the dresser style has continued. While other people threw up their arms in horror at the goings-on of outlaw motorcycle gangs, the American dresser clubs went on as they had always done. The dresser style is still in business, witness the latest Electra Glide.

Looking back through Harley's line-up over the years, the dresser, or the the basis for it, has always been there. The earliest dressers would have been side-valve V-twins. Then came the

Knuckleheads and, after the war, the FL/FLH Panheads and their subsequent manifestations as Hydra-Glide, Duo Glide and Electra Glide. They acquired fairings, panniers, stereos... The dresser lives on, and in factory-fresh form.

Mention the term custom bike today, though, and few people see a dresser. The usual image is a chopper, a rangy, raked-out object with long forks and high bars, the rider a laid-back, hairy rebel. Today, there are so many different styles of custom bike around that to see them all as choppers is like describing all pop music as rock-and-roll. Once upon a time, back in the late forties, things really were that simple. The new look, the antithesis of the dresser, was just starting then and, again, Harley was there first.

It began in California among the thousands of G.I.s who came back from the war to find life at home a little slow after all the fighting and flirting overseas. Their contemporaries who had stayed behind had mostly got wives and better jobs. Though U.S. industry had done well during the war too, jobs and prosperity were not available to everyone in 1945. There was the makings of a discontented group of people, unsettled and unemployed. Some of them had ridden bikes, Harley's WLAs, in uniform. They did what seems the obvious thing: they got on their bikes and hit the road. They formed groups, or gangs, very different from those of the clean-cut tourers. Pissed-Off Bastards, the name of one of the gangs, summed up the general mood pretty well. The usual weekend activity was to roar out of the city to wake up, not to say terrorize, the rural population.

Their bikes were invariably Harley or Indian V-twins, as these were both

OPPOSITE
A full-dresser Electra Glide at rest on Main Street, Sturgis.

ABOVE
A highly original-looking Duo Glide, 1959. Note the massive rear damper which formed part of the Duo's swinging-arm rear end. Some riders dismissed it but, except for hard-tail lovers among customizers, rear suspension was here to stay.

inexpensive and available. These bikes, and the Harley in particular since Indian was about to go into terminal fade-out, became known as outlaws' bikes. That was not quite accurate, since the traditional tourers were still riding around on fully

dressed Harleys, while the rebels customized their bikes into something quite different. Their motive was, partly perhaps, to distance themselves from the clubmen. More significantly, the standard Harleys of that time were lumbering, overweight beasts, as was emphasized by the newly arrved British imports. The little Triumph twins and Norton singles did not have the stamina of American bikes, but they were quick and nimble and, by comparison, the average big twin was a dinosaur.

As tuning was an expensive business largely confined to the race track, the answer was to quicken the Harley by getting rid of some of its excess poundage. All the touring gear was thrown away, followed by the front mudguard, a substantial piece of steel said to weigh as much as three Triumph Thunderbirds. When the rear mudguard was shortened, or 'bobbed', the bike became a California bobber. It looked much like the flat-track racers or hill climbers of the time but, more important, the bobber's stripped-down look was in tune with its riders' rough-and-ready image. Another Harley-Davidson look had arrived.

It might have remained no more than another California eccentricity, but for events at the small Californian town of Hollister on 4 July 1947. On that weeked a race approved by the AMA (American Motorcycle Association) was taking place, and 3,000 respectable clubmen turned up to watch. Less welcome arrivals were 500 or so unshaven bikers intent on having a roistering good time. Chaos ensued, though the mayhem reported by the local press seems to have been much exaggerated. Once *Life* magazine picked up the story of 4,000 bad bike bums with murder in their hearts, the true facts

respectable AMA about a 'one per cent minority', provided further encouragement. The more 'irresponsible' the chopped bikes and their riders became, the greater their attraction: rebellion was the point of the whole thing. Gangs formed all over the country with their own versions of the California bobber. Some even took to wearing 'One Percenter' patches. The battle of Hollister may have been no more than a minor skirmish, but it marked the beginning of the public image of the biker as rebel, an image permanently associated with the stripped-down Harley. To this day, Harley as the rebel's freedom machine still has its attraction, though the image is somewhat sanitized. The company is fully aware that this is part of what appeals to white-collar professionals who fancy a little weekend rebellion. Hollister may have been a blow to Harley's preferred image at the time, but the company has done well out of it ever since.

As the bobber, or chopper (the preferred term), grew in popularity, the style evolved. Longer forks, the chopper trademark, appeared in the 1950s. The reason for them is not clear. It may have been an imitation of the long, low drag bikes, which needed extended forks and stretched frames to keep the front wheel on the ground while roaring over the standing quarter-mile. According to another theory, the point of longer forks was to increase ground clearance. Harleys of the time were not built for rapid cornering, and the primary case would ground out long before that of, say, a Norton.

Whatever the motive, someone discovered that the springer forks from an old Harley VL were a good inch longer than standard. Better still, it turned out that standard Harley springers were identical in

LEFT
Contrasting custom styles at Sturgis: the red and black bike is a classic California bobber (bobbed rear mudguard, genuine hard-tail frame), but the flared and flamed bikes next to it belong to the 1990s.

ABOVE
On the road.

ceased to matter. Breathtaking tales of these marauding gangs with their hacked-about Harley-Davidsons spread across the country. The film director Stanley Kubrick became interested and *The Wild One* was the result. It helped to spread the word about the bad-boy bikers and prompted minor riots in many places where it was shown.

Condemnation by the police, press and parents, and the derisive comment by the

cross-section with the axle radius rods from a Ford car. Then, given a skilful welder, it was a simple matter to extend the forks more or less indefinitely. Once the demand was recognized, custom suppliers hastened to meet it. Jammer eventually offered a whole range of springers: 3-, 6-, 12-, 15- or 18-inches (45cm) over stock, all complete and ready to fit. Springers stayed in favour for a long while after Harley introduced telescopic forks in 1949. They were mechanically simpler and thus easier to extend, and their long, spindly appearance was in keeping with the average chopper. For some time springers were universally associated with the custom bike, one reason why Harley introduced its modern version in the late eighties. The Springer Softail was a tribute to postwar custom bikes as much as to pre-telescopic bikes in general.

With forks so long, it was natural to follow the two-wheel dragsters and rake them out. In fact it was necessary, or the whole bike would be pointing towards the sky. The headstock could be raked by cutting a piece out of the top tube of the frame, heating the headstock and bending it back before rewelding the frame, or by extending the downtube of the frame. Either method produced something close to the classic chopper profile.

There were many other possible developments. To match the forks, handlebars grew into buck horns, then high risers and finally ape hangers, while the pillion's sissy bar grew skywards to match them at the other end. This made the standard big touring fuel tank look incongruous, and it was reputedly racer Billy Kuber who replaced his KR's 4.5-gallon tank with one of 2.5 gallons from a Harley Hummer. The 125cc Hummer's

LEFT
Matt Grimwall was responsible for the paintwork on Richard Taylor's bike. It does its best to divert attention from the monster engine, but it's fighting a losing battle.

OPPOSITE
A nicely updated Electra Glide Shovelhead – this is a semi-stripped one which eschews all the usual fairings and screens, keeping just a simple pair of panniers. Note the modern stylized flame paint job.

much smaller tank opened up more air space and made the whole bike look leaner and more stripped-down. The tank from a Mustang moped had a similar effect as, to a lesser extent, did that from the then-new Sportster. As the supply of tanks made for other models was not inexhaustible, the custom specialists were soon making them from scratch.

They made a lot more than fuel tanks. A whole custom parts industry was growing up to supply innumerable details such as twisted foot rests, Maltese-Cross rear lights and swastika mirrors (some bikers fitted tiny dentist's mirrors, which complied with the letter of the law if not its spirit). The age of bolt-on customizing had arrived: seats, wheels, bars and levers could all be changed. Oil tanks could be hexagonal or cubical, and if the Hummer fuel tank seemed a bit boring, any number of specialists could provide one in the shape of a coffin. Entire custom frames – hard-tail, plungers, swinging-arm – appeared on the market, though some still preferred Harley's own 'straight-leg' frame for its simple elegance. Pattern engine parts had been available for some time, and it wasn't long before a complete 'Harley' could be built without using a single part from Milwaukee. It was even said to be possible to build a bike without using any American parts at all.

Some say that all this has little to do with genuine customizing. Certainly, if many owners are bolting on the same cheap trinket, they can't truly be said to be personalizing their bikes. Such arguments did not diminish the huge demand in the United States for custom parts, which allowed companies like Custom Chrome, Jammer, and Arlen Ness to grow and flourish. In the late 1960s, it was

predominantly for Harleys, the definitive custom bikes, that these accessories were produced, while in Britain, naturally enough, the custom scene was dominated by British twins.

This situation began to change at the end of the 1960s, when Japanese bikes were starting to make an impression, and not only in the moped class. Four-stroke fours from Honda and Kawasaki in particular offered better performance than any Harley ever had, and they were oil-tight, strong and affordable into the bargain. Soon, Jammer was offering 12-inch (30cm) over-forks for the Honda 4 as well as more traditional bikes. An editorial in *Chopper* magazine trumpeted, 'Hondas have taken over the chopper world, well at least at Daytona Beach this year.' The same issue discussed a new rigid frame designed for the Kawasaki Z1.

Could the customizers be turning away from Harley at last? They had some reason to do so. Riders of custom bikes need reliability as much as anyone else, and the Japanese were providing it. Besides, the Japanese fours had a visual appeal of their own, maybe not in profile, where they could not compete with the impressive mass of a V-twin, but from other angles the engine's

LEFT
*Chrome plating and a different paint job are
popular ways of transforming a big Harley.*

BELOW
*Ken Goldsbury on his 1972 Shovelhead,
'Barbarian'. In spite of high bars, small tank and
stepped seat, the standard rate means that it
stops short of being a full-blown chopper.*

FAR LEFT

A traditional mural on a fatbob tank with the usual suggestions of freedom, individualism and U.S. patriotism. Harley-Davidson has done well out of its association with the national eagle emblem.

LEFT

A custom Sportster shows what can be achieved with airbrush painting. Otherwise, this bike appears virtually standard.

RIGHT

Black, white and chrome make an interesting combination on this Softail. The colours may have changed, but flames and leather tassels are as popular as ever. Note the tiny, add-on indicator.

width and four chrome pipes were impressive. Something else was happening too. The custom bike was moving on.

By the early 1970s the classic high-barred chop had reached a dead end. There was a new emphasis on paint, especially flash metallics of lurid hue, on engraving, as a way of decorating parts that could not be painted, and on add-on parts. This was a long way from the original bobber, when the basic approach was to strip the bike down to bare essentials. Having followed that path until it went no farther, customizers devoted their efforts to gilding the lily.

New styles developed before stagnation set in. First were the low riders, which originated in the San Francisco Bay area. They reinvested the custom bike with the drag-strip look. Early choppers had of course been drag-inspired, but that was largely a matter of vague influence rather than direct imitation. Meanwhile, drag bikes had grown even longer and lower in pursuit of the fastest quarter-mile time. Grip was the limiting factor until Avon produced a wide, slick tyre specially designed for drag bikes. Although this gripped all right, it led to massive wheelies, and that was countered by making the bikes still lower to keep the front end on the tarmac. Lowriders tried to copy this look, being stretched and lowered until they resembled torpedoes on wheels, although performance was not the primary consideration. The bars were flat, not high-rise, and the rider stretched forward to grasp them rather than reclining as on the old, laid-back chopper. Since then, the lowrider has developed in two different directions: the original, long, slim look usually with a hard-tail frame, raked forks and pulled-back bars, and a shorter,

RIGHT
The Husteads' store is obviously a favourite stopping place for Harley riders during the Sturgis meeting. Not a car in sight!

OPPOSITE
An evocative scene among Daytona's palms, with nice engine detailing on the bike and a Faustian mural worth close examination.

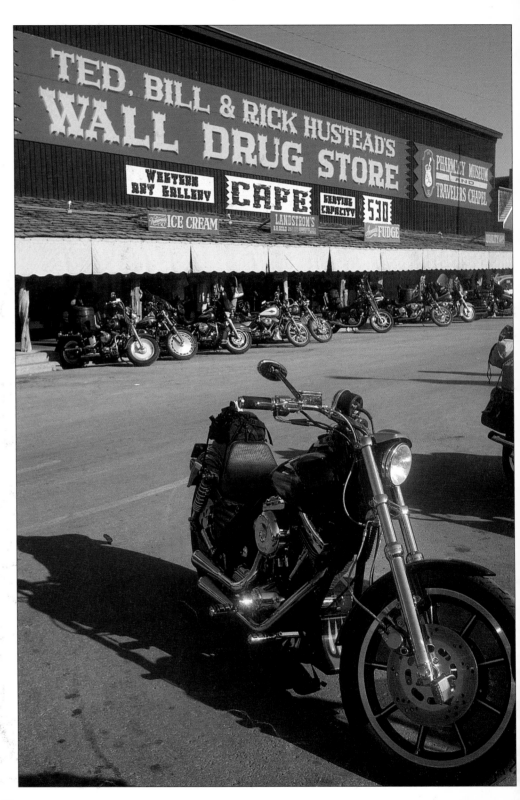

stubbier look, still close to the ground but with a rounded tank and shortened, standard-rake forks. The bad news for Harley was that its tall V-twin was unsuited to the lowrider look. All the same, it was soon to make a comeback as the favourite U.S. custom bike.

Before that happened, there was another development. The era of the custom-bike show arrived. They proliferated throughout the seventies, with every bike builder trying to outshine everyone else in pursuit of a prize. Year after year the bikes became ever more outrageous – chops with forks so long they looked about to bend in the middle, twin-engined monsters with nowhere for the rider to sit. Builders began to put together custom bikes purely for shows, with no intention of riding them. They could be trailered to an event, wheeled onto a plinth and, having with luck collected the prize, trailered home again, never moving an inch under their own power.

This somewhat grotesque situation eventually provoked a backlash. Today, the Kent Custom Show insists that no bike can be entered for a prize unless it is actually ridden at the show, and the custom-bike movement has accepted that a bike is not a bike unless it can be ridden. The latest creations put more emphasis on visual impact and fine technical detail rather than trying to be the most outrageously weird object on show.

The world would be a duller place without show bikes, and it is worth taking a closer look at one or two of them.

Arlen Ness is one of the best-known names in the custom parts business. He started out making custom handlebars of his own design and grew with the industry. He now employs thirty people and produces countless lines of expensive, high-quality parts, many of them for export and all of them for Harleys exclusively. The first bike he ever worked on was his own Knucklehead, and he sees no reason to diversify. He also produces show bikes. He claims he enjoys it, and no one could doubt it, though of course they also generate useful publicity for the Arlen Ness business. A striking bike exhibited at all the big custom shows throughout the year will be seen by thousands – a long-running, high-impact advertisement.

'Two Bad' was a notable example. It did not really look like a motorcycle at all, apparently consisting of two big engines slung between a pair of wheels, with serpentine exhaust and intake pipes swirling here and there. Ground clearance was to be measured in millimetres rather than inches, and a large twin-throat carburettor gaped open-mouthed an inch or two above the floor. Both engines were 883 Sportster units opened up to 1000cc, and were supercharged as well. They were connected to each other by a substantial toothed belt. To show them off to good effect, the fuel tank was built into the rear of the long, low frame, and of course anything that could not be painted was either gold-plated or engraved, or both. Was Two Bad ever actually ridden? History does not record.

The Ferrari bike is a nineties version of a similar thing, no less outrageous in its own way but fully rideable, although it's not the sort of bike for popping down to the shops. Like several modern bikes, it adopts full bodywork, though fortunately not enclosing the engine, and a Ferrari theme, from the bright red paint to the Testarossa-style air intakes. The aluminium body was shaped by Craig Naff, according to Arlen

Ness's ideas, though it's a far cry from the slim low riders Ness was once associated with. It has to be rather wide to accomodate the massive 265/60 rear tyre. There is just one engine, although at 2.1 litres it has the capacity of two normal ones. Each cylinder is fed by a Magnusson supercharger and two Dell' Orto carburettors. If that lot won't get you past the car in front, there's nitrous on tap as well. The Ferrari bike certainly draws the crowds.

OPPOSITE
Sturgis was once in the heart of Indian country. This tank illustrates an appropriate theme.

BELOW
High-rise bars are making something of a comeback on the contemporary custom Harley, combined on this one with a very low-riding rear end.

An all-red, stretched Evo, owned by Jim Randolph. The heads have been painted to match the rest of the bike, quite a common technique today, while the front end is pure, skeletal chopper.

Chapter Five
Custom Harleys: a Renaissance

RIGHT
A 'British' Harley. Goodman Engineering made replicas of the legendary Norton frame and fitted some of them with Sportster Evo V-twin engines – beautiful!

BELOW
Not one but two six-pot callipers haul down the speed of Richard Taylor's latest show bike.

Custom bikes in the late 1970s were a mass of chrome, engraving and a general excess of bad taste, and the Harley hegemony had been lost. In the new decade, a general revival took place. For a start, Harleys came back into fashion as the first choice of U.S. custom builders. In Britain and Europe too, professionals often chose Harleys.

The Evolution engine, the basis of Harley's renaissance, was largely responsible for this return to favour. Ostensibly just a new top-end design on the old Shovelhead, it was in fact a big step forward in all respects. Reliable, oil-tight and well-behaved, it brought quality, for so many years an elusive ingredient, back into factory-built Harleys. Its launch in 1983 came shortly after another milestone in H-D history, the management buy-out from AMF. The AMF era had not been all bad by any means. It left a legacy of fresh investment and high production. Newly independent, Harley-Davidson was free to pursue its own recovery. The only prerequisite was to get the product right.

From the point of view of the customizers, it did, and not only by making more reliable motorcycles. It had taken H-D a long time to realise that the custom movement, particularly in America, was

part of its life blood. At one time the company wanted nothing to do with those unshaven fellows who chopped their bikes about, removed the silencers and roared around the country giving motorcycling in general, and Harley-Davidson in particular, a bad name. They represented a total contradiction of the clean-cut sportsman image that Harley had worked long and hard to foster. Many Harley dealers refused to service machines that had been customized.

This attitude had to change. That it did was largely due to Willie G. Davidson, grandson of the first William. He was a genuine biking enthusiast who fortuitously held an influential position in the styling department. His FX Super Glide of 1970 was a parts-bin special – a collection of existing parts combined to form a new model. But the bulky big twin married to a skinny Sportster front end added up to more than the sum of its parts. It had mildly chopped styling, and an eye-catching white, red and blue colour scheme. The customers loved it. Then there was the FXS Lowrider of 1977, which advanced a stage further: longer wheelbase, low, 27-inch (67cm) seat, two-into-one exhaust, flat handlebars. It was really an updated chopper/low rider, but straight from the

factory. It too was a great success and, at a time when the traditional big twins were languishing, soon became Harley's best seller.

Harley needed no more encouragement. The introduction in 1980 of belt final drive was celebrated by the all-black Sturgis (another Sturgis emerged ten years later to celebrate the fiftieth anniversary of Black Hills). The company was also adopting a higher corporate profile at the main public events, including Sturgis and Daytona. Willie G. became its roving ambassador, out on two wheels in leather jacket and jeans at events all over the country. There was the Evo launch ride, when the company president and the managing director rode new bikes to Daytona, and the buy-back ride, when a group of top managers celebrated the company's regained independence by riding from York, the AMF base in Pennsylvania, to the old H-D works in Milwaukee. The new spirit was summed up in the advertising slogan of 1982, 'Motorcycles by the People, for the People'. Since then, bikes that trade on Harley's custom heritage, the Wide Glide, Softail and others, have become mainstays of the range. Harley-Davidson has become an example to others in the art of the factory custom.

Harley had become street-wise, recognizing where most of its customers were coming from. Whether its pro-custom policy sprang from genuine enthusiasm for the product or was simply a piece of cunning corporate PR, the effect was the same. Harley-Davidson moved closer to its customers, gained in credibility, and sold more bikes as a result.

But there were other reasons why the customizers became convinced that

LEFT
Whether or not that was its main purpose, Richard Taylor's bike has done well at shows – second prize at Genk in Belgium in 1995, best in show in Kent, England, the same year.

RIGHT
Power? Richard Taylor estimates 150bhp from this twin supercharged bike, which has valves the size of dinner plates. When the photograph was taken the bike was not yet run in, but Richard says he does use it on the road now and again.

LEFT
A more typical modern custom Harley, based like many others on a Softail Evo. Weber carburettor, almost-flat bars and billet accessories mark it as contemporary.

OPPOSITE
This typical, strikingly bright, modern paintwork is far from the once-obligatory 'medievalist' mural. Here again the painter has felt free to produce a new variation of the Harley-Davidson logo.

Harleys were once more worthy of their craft. Of course Harleys are, and always have been, large and imposing machines. They give the customizer a larger canvas to work on. But there was a special reason for their renewed appeal. The Evo was increasingly a rarity among large motorcycle engines in being air-cooled. More and more of the latest units are liquid-cooled, because that is the easiest way to keep a high-performance engine quiet and reliable. Technically, that's fine, but the loss of those evocative fins tends to turn the engine, visually, into an uninteresting block of metal. Hidden behind the bodywork of a modern bike, its appearance doesn't matter, but exposed on a custom bike, the modern engine simply looks boring. Some manufacturers have resorted to fake fins, an unsatisfying expedient, like putting Gothic spires on a power station. On a Harley, by contrast, the look of the engine, all finned and polished alloy, is a major contributor to its visual appeal.

It is more than a coincidence that while Harley-Davidson has been renewing itself, so has the custom bike. Each stimulates the other. New styles and influences have appeared, which have attracted new talent and new ideas. Equally desirable, there is also more money. The modern custom bike is a far more sophisticated animal than its predecessors, with advances in welding, paint and tuning in particular. A new breed of wealthy customer does not mind paying a lot of money for someone else to build the ultimate bike. The custom specialists, both builders and parts makers, have profited accordingly, and that in turn encourages a healthier industry, with more choice available.

Paint has developed technically as well

LEFT
Serious tuning on this Evo, at Daytona in 1994, is suggested by the supercharger, down-draught twin-choke carb and four valve heads, not to mention the parts you can't see.

OPPOSITE
Subtle engine painting and ghosted flames work well on this neat, clean custom at the Boardwalk show in Daytona. Twin front discs are a common modification.

RIGHT
Another Boardwalk bike extends the single colour theme to almost every part. Modern paints and powder coating allow deep, rich finishes on parts that previously could not be painted at all.

FAR RIGHT
CNC-produced billet parts, carved from solid chunks of alloy, feature on this bike. Billet handlebar grips are very common now, and this one also has a mirror stem and foot rests made in the same way.

as in terms of style. There is a mind-boggling array of shades available, and they are more durable than the metal-flakes of old. The airbrush opened up a whole new field of custom painting, known as murals. Its fine control allowed incredibly lifelike detail, and no custom bike of the seventies was complete without a semi-naked woman holding slavering hounds on a leash. Subjects have become more sophisticated since, although there is still a good quota of topless she-devils, and those perennial favourites, flames and skulls, associated with the danger element in motorcycling, will always be with us. What is new is the popularity of purely abstract patterns. Custom bikes don't need to be harbingers of doom any more. Bright candy-colours and cool pastels are just as popular today, and the subject matter of murals can include anything under the sun (or beyond it). The important factor is its uniqueness to the owner. It doesn't really matter if bystanders don't understand what it means. It is often something personal to the individual who thought of it. That's what customizing is all about.

Chrome and engraving are still present, but they are used far more sparingly now. Engraving used to be the means of decorating those parts that could not be painted. It was an art in itself: a craftsman like Don Bloxidge made a living engraving guns and jewellery before the English customizer, John Reed, persuaded him to try bikes. But engraving was often overdone. There was a limit to what it could achieve, apart from nice swirly patterns. Modern powder coating, however, means that engine and transmission can be finished in any solid colour required, whether matching the rest of the bike, as in some bodywork bikes, or complementing it.

LEFT

If you can't afford it, or don't want to go in for raking, stretching and fancy paintwork, a Live To Ride air-cleaner is the next best thing – or so thousands of Harley owners seen to think.

RIGHT

Like many modern custom bikes, as much work here has gone into components as into the bike's appearance. The engine has been balanced and blueprinted, with nitrous injection and twin plug heads to help things along.

The trend of the nineties seems to be away from fussy detailing. As in other art forms, the secret is not only to have a good idea of what you want to achieve in the first place, but to know when to stop. Garish gold plating has been largely replaced by billet aluminium parts. In fact, if anything typifies the modern custom bike, or at least those with well-heeled owners, it is the billet part. The advent of CNC milling machines has made a whole range of parts possible: handlebar grips, wheels, foot rests, all carved from solid chunks of aluminium alloy. Small batches can be made at reasonable cost, and very accurately too. They can be anodized in any colour, but many people prefer to leave them as polished aluminium for that 'precision-engineering' look.

Engineering plays a larger part in creating the custom Harley than it used to. That may reflect the speediness of other bikes, or simply that there's only so much you can spend on a paint job. It is not necessarily the case that owners actually contemplate using all the extra power. Like the thousands of car drivers who happily buy 4 x 4 vehicles and never venture off-

RIGHT
The rear of Mallard Teal's café. The chrome bottle is not a soda syphon: it supplies a nitrous-injection system for use when Mallard hears a Kawasaki coming past!

OPPOSITE
Chris Le Sauvage's FXR at Daytona Beach. The different shades of a single colour are attractive, but Paulita Coronado and Josie Ameredo do their best to put it in the shade – literally.

road, they like to know the hardware is there. For whatever reason, serious engine work is now common. It ranges from a freer-flowing air filter to a complete custom-built engine (as with any other part of the bike, it is possible to build a power unit with no Harley parts at all). The standard 80ci (1311cc) Harley engine gives about 70bhp at the flywheel, but it is fairly easy to raise it to well over 100bhp with readily available parts. Sportsters, too, have the potential for big power hikes: the conversion from 883 to 1200 has always been popular and is fairly straightforward.

To begin with, many are happy with a simple bolt-on conversion, such as an after-market carburettor from S & S. The Super E offers an accelerator pump for better throttle response and is a bigger carburettor than the standard Keihin. For higher performance, the 40mm Dell' Orto unit's big advantage is twin chokes (the standard Harley is almost unique among motorcycles in having only one single-choke carb to serve its big engine). With fuel injection now making its appearance on production Harleys, the end of the after-market carb may be in sight, but meanwhile it remains the easiest route to a horsepower boost. Cams are relatively easy to change as well. A vast number are available from Sifton, S & S, Crane, Andrews and others, all with their own ranges from mild to race level.

For the ultimate in power, the whole engine needs attention. Bore and stroke kits, including flywheels, pistons and connecting rods, expand the typical big twin from 74/80ci (1213/1311cc) to 96 ci (1573cc) or even more. There is little point in spending a lot of money on the bottom end without doing the same at the top. The standard heads can be ported and polished

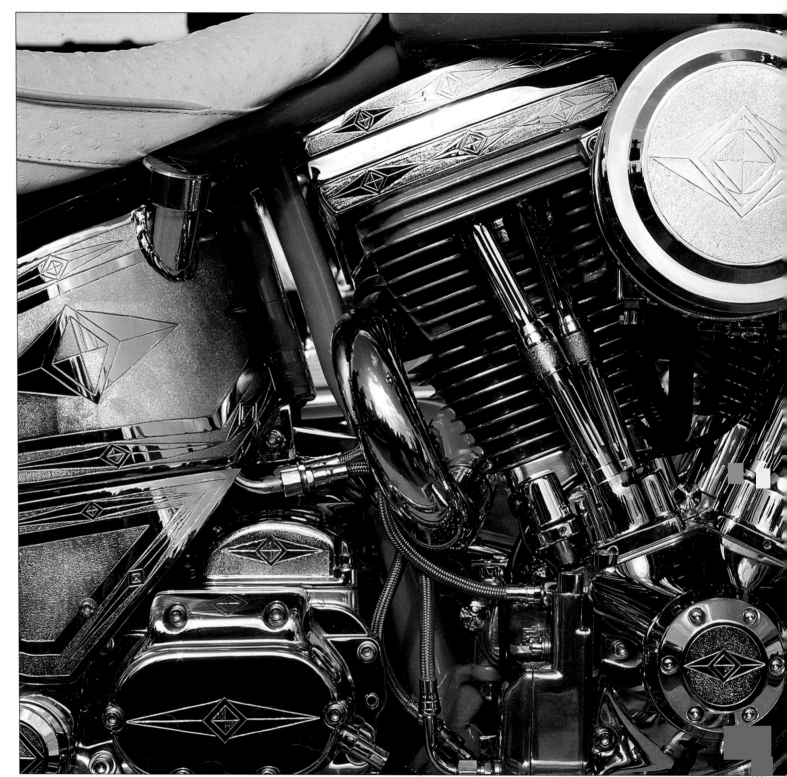

and fitted with bigger valves. More radically, four-valve heads can be substituted. If that is not enough, turbocharging and supercharging represent the ultimate in tuning. Yet, in spite of all this expensive power boosting, the impression remains that most bike builders make these modifications primarily for the sake of a more impressive appearance.

With so much power available, it is fortunate that brakes have advanced too. They have always been a favourite part to change among customizers, as the standard Harley brakes not only look rather puny but are in reality none too powerful. Favoured replacements are four- or six-pot calipers from Performance Machine or Billet. An alternative, though one that is not simple to carry out, is to fit the entire front end from a Japanese sports bike. That provides twin disc brakes, modern alloy wheels and forks, and maybe also anti-dive, adjustable damping and pre-load. It is a high-tech approach which so far has found more favour in Europe than the United States, but for a Harley custom with 1990s brakes and handling, it is probably the best procedure.

As new techniques and new ideas permeate the custom-bike movement, styles inevitably follow them. The basic rule these days is that there are no rules! If your idea of a custom Harley is a duotone Heritage Softail, fine. A street-racerized Sportster? That's fine too. Even if it is a high-barred, metal-flaked and engraved chopper in true 1970s style, no one will turn a hair. These days, anything is acceptable. The only limiting factors are cash and imagination.

On the whole, this is a very healthy situation. With everyone open to new ideas, customizing is unlikely to stagnate.

LEFT
You have to look closely to see the engraving on this Evo, but the closer you look, the more diamonds you find. The effect is less cluttered than the curlicues of early custom engraving.

ABOVE
There are some riders even at Daytona who like to keep their bikes, like this stock Sportster, as they were when they left the factory.

One drawback is that it is becoming more and more difficult to categorize customs. Gone are the days when the Americans built choppers and the British-built café racers. Now, many builders feel free to mix and match between any number of styles, and the categories, insofar as they ever existed, are becoming ever more blurred.

Take the street racer, or café, a popular type of the last few years. Part lowrider, part café racer, it has become the performance bike among Harley customs. It is long and low, but not slim like the original low riders. The frame will be stretched, perhaps raked as well, but the forks are likely to be standard length. Bars are either straight or pulled back, to avoid too much of a racing crouch, but definitely not high-rise. Sissy bars are out too: most street racers are solo seaters in any case. A headlamp fairing is common and, of all Harley customs, these are most likely to be given a high-tech Japanese front end. They are not to be confused with the barrel-chested, all-black street fighter that is popular in Europe, especially Britain, today but hardly ever seen in the United States.

Harleys lend themselves especially well to nostalgia customs, largely because the engine has looked much the same for generations. The modern springer forks and Softail frame also offer the means to build an ersatz old bike. Many riders don't bother with frame or engine, as it is possible to make almost any Harley look old simply by bolting on appropriate parts. Headlamp shrouds, studded-leather saddlebags (shades of the old dresser look), whitewall tyres and fishtail silencers are all available off the shelf. Lawayne Matthies' Xzotic Cycle Products specializes in items to make a new Harley look older and markets a kit to turn any Evolution

LEFT
This custom makes several nods to the past, from the raked frame to the flames on the small tank. These days many painters prefer ghosted flames for a more subtle effect that rewards a second look.

RIGHT
An attractive pair of his-and-her matched bikes with reversed colour schemes. The tank logo is based on the art deco device adopted by Harley-Davidson in the 1930s, which moved the company on from the image of the Silent Gray Fellow.

engine into an apparent Panhead. The replacement Panhead rocker cover simply bolts on. Old-style ribbed covers hide the modern electronic ignition. Even Arlen Ness has got in on the act. To publicize his new Taildragger mudguard, he built Flamin' Ape, a bike that was low and drag-tailed at the back but featured classic ape-hanger bars and after-market springer forks up front. The paintwork displayed retro-look flames, of course.

Nostalgia is also the main inspiration for the luxury liners, or bodywork bikes. One stylistic influence is the led sled custom cars with their enclosed wheels and ground-hugging shape. The bodywork flows eloquently from headstock to rear mudguard – the antithesis of the lean and hungry chopper. The massive mudguards are clearly inspired by those of the last Indian Chiefs (much more stylish than the equivalent Harley FL), and the same theme is followed throughout. Solid wheels (the Fatboy was the first Harley production bike to have them) are used to emphasize the all-in-one-piece appearance, which is usually also enhanced by one dark, solid colour with subtle chrome highlighting, and headlamp set in a nacelle. So far, most builders have resisted the temptation to cover up the engine, since that big hunk of polished alloy is still the centre of any custom bike.

One custom builder, Bob Dron, who also runs the big H-D dealership in Oakland, has made liners a speciality. His Heritage Royale won a major prize at the 1992 Oakland Roadster show. It was followed by the purple Heritage II, whose most striking feature was twin headlights each set in its own shroud.

America may lead the way in custom bikes but, curiously enough, the only

LEFT
This looks like a well-used bike (the chain certainly needs adjusting). It is typical of the more everyday bikes present by the thousand at Sturgis.

RIGHT.
Cruising the beach, helmetless, is one of the main attractions at Daytona, perhaps a little too popular these days. Watch out for the surfboards...

PAGE 90
Crawfish and funnel cakes are Sturgis specialities, and if they aren't, they should be.

PAGE 91
A French-registered 1940 Knucklehead sidecar outfit receiving customary attention on the Isle of Man seafront. Before the days of rear suspension, most passengers preferred a 'chair' to squatting on a hard-tail.

country to have a style named after it is Sweden. The small number of bikes in Sweden, where the winter is long and the season for riding consequently short, does not suggest that it is promising territory. But maybe those long, dark, winter months ensconced in the workshop explain why Swedish chops often turn out so well. Swedish-style bikes, whether built there or not, are neat, clean and uncluttered, with no extraneous cables, pipes or wires to be seen. The colour scheme augments this look, being often one solid colour with no excessive chrome or engraving. Long forks are virtually compulsory. A Swedish Harley actually holds what must be the world record for fork length at 236 inches and, yes, they did bend in the middle! Most riders opt for a modest 20-24 inches over stock, with a low-riding, hard-tail rear end. Here, if anywhere, the chopper survives in a form akin to the original.

French riders have a different approach. They go for more instant appeal and style, in the manner of Odessey Kolour's Fat Slug, a luxury liner in pastel green. In Germany, customizing is more problematic because of strict type-approval regulations, which means that quick, bolt-on devices are less favoured. It is often worth using an older machine as the basis, because they are easier to get through the necessary TUV (annual vehicle fitness) test. As for the Dutch, anyone who believes they have no sense of humour should take a look at Hans Boekhoue's Shovelhead. It is a bright yellow blob of a machine, hardly recognizable as a motorbike, let alone a Harley. Liberal splashes of lime green, purple and metal-flake red turn it into something that looks more like a high-tech jukebox. The Italians, who after all have their own V-twins, are less keen on

Harleys, and in Britain Triumphs are the favourite chop material. The custom scene there is so varied that it is impossible to make generalizations, but Harleys are certainly involved. They may not be the first choice for customizers in all other countries as they are in the United States, but what does exist everywhere is great variety and vitality. For custom bikes, those are the characteristics that count.

Not everyone has the time, inclination or – let's face it – the ability to build his own custom bike, but he may well have a clear idea of what he wants. That is where the professional builders come in. In America there are hundreds of them, most specializing in Harleys to a greater or lesser extent. Some may be painters by trade, others tuners, and there are plenty whose welding skills lead them to concentrate on frame modifications. Some are allrounders, like Arlen Ness, who started off with paintwork but progressed into bodywork and parts design. Naturally, the custom builders form a fairly close community. Everyone meets up at the big shows at least once during the year, and it's not uncommon to find a bike that has been worked on by several different experts: engine by one, paint by another, body by a third, and so on. What unites them all is their commitment to the custom Harley.

The name of Arlen Ness crops up time and again in the world of custom bikes. If history had been different, he might have stuck with the day job, while custom-painting cars in his spare time. Fortunately for Harley owners everywhere, he bought a Knucklehead, found people liked the way he had painted it, and eventually went to work on bikes full-time. Actually, much of Arlen's time has been spent producing parts rather than whole bikes. He started by

designing a pair of bars, Ramhorns, that sold well enough to persuade him to continue this side of the business. It made his fortune, literally. The Arlen Ness parts trade is now very big, exporting parts all over the world.

Moustachioed Dave Perewitz typifies the attitude of most professional bike builders. 'What I want to do,' he says, 'is build bikes, pay my bills – and have fun doing it.' With his brother Donnie, Dave has been painting and building bikes since he left school. They began in a shed behind the house, though Cycle Fabrications, or CycleFab, has since moved into a building with a little more space. Unlike Arlen Ness, Dave still builds complete bikes for some customers, besides simple jobs like installing bolt-on parts. Like all builders, he has his own pet projects too. At the fiftieth Sturgis he had a Harley with a twin-carburettor Evolution engine, a Ness frame and (a Perewitz trademark) a flaming paint job.

It is surprising how many of the professionals learned their trade by simply practising it, with only natural talent and an eye for style to support their accumulating experience. Ron Simms, who is based in Hayward east of San Francisco Bay, is therefore something of an exception, since he sports degrees in mechanical engineering and architecture – an excellent combination of function and form well suited to the world of custom bikes. His machines are usually fat, low and wide. When most builders were extending the forks in the early seventies, Ron Simms' bikes often had under-stock forks and decreased rake. He also seems to have anticipated the move towards billet aluminium parts, fabricating some triple trees years before billets were widely used. His Bay Area

Custom Cycles currently lists 800 bolt-on billet parts, all for Harleys.

Many builders prefer bikes with immediate, obvious impact. Don Hotop is more interested in detail. The machines that come out of his workshop are low and understated. Some look quite close to stock, but when examined more closely the carefully worked-out detail can be appreciated. Like many others, he began building bikes in the evenings, going full-time when a good opportunity arose. One recent Hotop FXR appears very mild, but the frame was cut into no less than eight pieces before it was reassembled the way he wanted it. Details like cable clamps and brackets are machined from stainless steel by hand. It's impossible to imagine Don Hotop fitting an off-the-shelf part.

All these builders have been in the business for years, but Mike and Felix La Fore are younger. Another partnership of brothers have their shop in Lakewood, Colorado where they build a wide variety of bikes, although they like to specialize in what they call café sport (the café, or street racer, described above), low to the ground, with a little headlamp fairing. One of their most notable bikes, though not in that category, is the all-black Evo built for tatooist Thomas Dias, in which the derby and inspection covers in the primary case are designed to spin round while the engine is running. The influx of new talent into the custom-bike business, as exemplified by the La Fore brothers, is a sure sign of a healthy future. There are of course countless other builders and painters who produce high-quality work: Rick Doss, Starr (one of the few women in the business), Bob Dron, Pat Kennedy, Al Reichenbach... The list goes on, and, with the custom scene as lively as it is today, it's likely to keep growing.

The ultra-modern paint job leads one to expect an Evolution Softail underneath, but Tom Fedorowski's bike is actually a much older Shovelhead.

Chapter Six
Getting Together

Like others who share a minority interest, people who ride motorcycles like to get together. It might be to watch racing, play silly games, get drunk, or just to talk about bikes. This has long been part and parcel of owning a motorcycle, and it is as true of Harley-Davidson riders as anyone else.

The rallies and runs organized by the factory-sponsored Harley Owners Group (HOG) have spread all over the world. No other motorcycle manufacturer plays such an active role in encouraging social activities, and as they have spread, they have become better organized. They have also grown big – very big. The chief motorcycle gatherings in the United States attract more people than rock concerts, political demos, carnivals, or any comparable event. The numbers at Sturgis or Daytona are measured not in hundreds or thousands, but in hundreds of thousands.

This is a recent development. Both Sturgis and Daytona are long-established – well past their fiftieth anniversaries. Both started as low-key races organized by local bikers for their own amusement. Both have become, in effect, massive gatherings of Harley owners, although officially anyone can come, and in recent years attendance

has rocketed. Until Sturgis was 'discovered' by *Easyriders* magazine in 1978, a few thousand bikers would turn up once a year and stay for a few days, but in 1979 the visitors numbered 25,000 and ten years later there were more like 100,000. In 1990, when the Black Hills Motor Classic celebrated its fiftieth anniversary, twice that number turned up before the official start. The final total was about half a million, which is about 100 times the town's resident population.

Most of these people were mounted on Harleys and, even if they did not all ride them there, they would never have dreamed of arriving on anything else. The exploding numbers reflected the worldwide fascination with Harley, and included the growing band of Harley leisure riders, relatively well-off born-again bikers to whom motorcycling was a weekend hobby rather than a standard means of transport. To such people, riding, or transporting, the shiny new V-Twin to Daytona or Sturgis was an attractive trip, and perhaps they also liked the idea of meeting others with a touch of the loner and the rebel in their bones. It seemed more fun than a weekend in Palm Springs or a seven-day package tour of Europe.

A visit to any of the big events reveals

LEFT
Still life in a Black Hills camp site.

ABOVE
Cruising in 100 degrees of heat near Rapid City, South Dakota.

the variety of people who go to them. There are enough tattoos and unkempt beards to show that the old school of 'real' bikers is here. These are not attorneys from Des Moines but people who ride their bike day in and day out, to whom iowning a bike is more than a hobby and much more than mere transport. As Sturgis and Daytona have grown, they have attracted people who have been riding Harleys for years and going to local, rather than national, rallies. But the main point is that these thousands of riders from vastly different backgrounds and with vastly different outlooks on life get along together very well. There's no friction, no trouble. The atmosphere is one of tolerance, in which everyone can do more or less what he or she likes without antagonizing anyone else. It's what they have in common (even if they share nothing else) that draws them together. They all love bikes, and they all love Harleys.

Sturgis

Sturgis, South Dakota, is classed as a city but it's really a small town. Until the Rapid City Motorcyclists started an annual race meeting in the 1930s, it seemed destined to slumber on for ever, a quiet backwater in the Black Hills. It had known exciting times in the past. Originally, it was a Gold Rush town, springing up to service the needs of 19th-century prospectors, and was by all accounts, like most frontier towns, a little on the wild side. 'Wild Bill' Hickok was killed in nearby Deadwood, and General Custer made his last stand on the Little Bighorn not far away. As the gold petered out and the frontier moved on, law and order were gradually established and Sturgis became respectable.

Respectable and, for J.C. 'Pappy' Hoel, who rode an Indian and was a prominent member of the local bike club in the 1930s, a shade too boring. For their own entertainment, Pappy and his friends set about organizing their own races. At Sturgis there was an old, overgrown, oval circuit of about half a mile, called the Fairgrounds, which had not been used for perhaps twenty years. They cleared it up and, in 1936, held the first races. Two years later they gained AMA approval, and the Black Hills Motor Classic became an annual, official fixture, which has continued ever since, uninterrupted except for a short break during World War II.

Besides the racing, the club, renamed the Jackpine Gypsies Motorcycle Club, organized a parade through the town, with awards for Best Dressed Rider and Best Turned Out Club: those were the days when the clubs prided themselves on their smart, buttoned-up turnout. Sturgis soon became much more than just another race meeting.

As word got around, the meeting expanded. What attracted people was not the hope of winning the prize for Best Dressed Rider. For many of them Sturgis, roughly halfway between the Great Lakes and the Pacific, was relatively accessible, at least by comparison with Daytona or Laconia. Besides, Sturgis offered the romance of an old Wild West town. Like the gunslingers of old, the bikers rode into town, hitched their mounts outside the saloon and, when it was time to go, headed out on the lonesome trail once more, into the wide open plains under the big sky. That was the image anyway. It still attracts thousands.

Today, the town welcomes its 'cowboys'. The residents have grown accustomed to the annual invasion, when the town is swamped by bikers, who outnumber them by thousands. They also

RIGHT

Main Street, Sturgis. This is one of the quieter moments. At the evening peak or during the huge ride out, bikes are nose to tail from one end of the street to the other.

OPPOSITE

As these riders discovered, it's a long way from New York to Sturgis, but worth the journey.

hope to profit, for the meeting is a massive money spinner. For one week in the year, shops that usually mend shoes or sell doughnuts are rented out to traders with goods designed to appeal to bikers. Shop signs on Main Street are hastily covered by banners for ABATE (the U.S. riders' rights association), for Big Daddy's infamous T-shirts, for sellers of leather goods and tattoo parlours. There are countless things to buy – mugs, toys, official Sturgis beer, even Christmas trees. Covered accommodation is impossible to find unless booked a year or so in advance. Instead, the riders pitch tents. At the fiftieth Classic, 19 separate camp sites were set up, all crammed with tents and Harleys. Sadly, Pappy Hoel was not there. After fifty years of involvement with the Sturgis meeting, he died shortly before the Classic began.

He did live more than long enough the see his home town totally reorganized for the needs of visiting bikers. They have replaced the prospectors who, 150 years ago, supported the town in much the same way. Peaceable citizens of those days would perhaps prefer the bikers, as Sturgis during the Classic is a more law-abiding place than it was in the bad old days. Not that the Classic was so peaceful when the 'One Percenters' came to town, upsetting the locals and the smart AMA clubmen alike. Camp sites were burned, there were many arrests, and the whole scene became more than fraught. But in time everyone came to realise that a more co-operative attitude would benefit all, and that has prevailed ever since.

The original purpose of Sturgis, the racing, still goes on. Apart from the old half-mile oval at the Fairgrounds, there is drag racing, vintage TT and the Jackpine

Gypsies hill climb. But the racing is not the centre of events any more. That is to be found in Main Street, where the riders with their bikes gather to chew the fat, see and be seen, or just sit in the sun. The Hell's Angels and the Bandidos rub shoulders with the born-again bikers from Des Moines. The Bikers for Jesus are here, so are the Women in the Wind, the Vietnam Vets and the HOGs. They are all here to celebrate the same thing, which effectively unites half a million souls. The atmosphere is not unlike the legendary hippy pop festivals of the sixties, when love and peace were supposed to overcome all human differences. Only here the bond is Harley-Davidson, and it seems to work just as well as flower power.

The bikes reflect as much variety as the people – not a lot of different makes, but lots of different Harley-Davidsons. Sportsters, Glides (Wide, Electra, Ultra, Hydra), in fact practically everything that has come out of the factory since the four founders first set up shop, all are here. Being Harleys, few of them look as they did at the dealer's. Most are customized in one way or another, if only with a Live to Ride air-cleaner box or a set of handlebar tassels. Others are completely transformed, as genuine custom-built bikes. There are bikes with two engines or three wheels, low riders and high-barred choppers, supercharged dragsters and tatty rat bikes that have never seen a tube of Autosol. What cannot be seen are many Japanese bikes. There may be a small handful of Harley look-alikes, Vulcan V-twins and Honda Goldwings, but they are exceptions. Sturgis is about Harley-Davidson.

If sitting on Main Street watching the bikes rumble slowly past begins to pall (the procession can degenerate into an almighty two-wheel traffic jam), there is plenty going on elsewhere. The Buffalo Chip camp ground is virtually an event in itself. Covering the best part of 500 acres (200 hectares), it has its own newspaper, radio station, and live music on stage every night. It is also one of the wilder parts of Sturgis. The amount of naked flesh, especially female, on view here would mean arrest on Main Street. But, as in the rest of this giant jamboree, there is very little trouble. The bikers are here for enjoyment, not aggravation.

People have unexpected reasons for coming to Sturgis. Amazingly, some seem to come to get married. In 1990 Sturgis City Council issued 99 marriage licences to couples who chose to take the plunge during the Classic. A more likely motive is to take advantage of the superb riding country of the Black Hills. With the vast numbers now involved, the big ride out has become more of a shuffle: forward a few feet, stop and wait, a few feet more, stop again, and so on. It's an astonishing sight, and probably unique, but for real riding it makes more sense to go singly or in small groups. Exciting roads swoop through magnificent scenery, with natural attractions like the Thunderhead Falls. On the more conventional tourist trail, Deadwood has become a Wild West parody in Disneyland style, and Mount Rushmore displays the gigantic stone heads of four outstanding U.S. presidents. According to rumour, a confederation of HOGs is planning to commission a similar monument featuring William Harley and the Davidson brothers. Stranger things have happened!

Daytona

Daytona Beach is an upmarket Florida seaside resort with a Hilton hotel where the clientele are quite unlike the occupants of the average Sturgis guest house, whether in Bike Week or not. It's a very different kind of town from Sturgis, and Daytona Bike Week is different from the Sturgis Classic. It is more controlled, less like a week-long party; colours are banned from the bars (they are everywhere in Sturgis). The Rat's Hole custom show, reputedly the biggest in the world, is the scene of very serious competition for prestigious awards. To win at the Rat's Hole confers a great deal of kudos on owner, bike and builder.

Yet the two events have much in common. Both have grown from low-key races into huge festivals attended by Harley riders from all over the world. Conveniently, Daytona takes place in the first week in March while Sturgis is in August, so the keenest enthusiasts can go to both.

Whereas Pappy Hoel and his friends restored an old oval track, the Daytona races started on the flat, sandy beach, 25 miles (40km) long and 500 feet (150m) wide at low tide, which attracts so many other people to this sunny resort. In the old days, Harley WRs would battle it out with Norton Internationals in the classic 200-mile (320km) race over the sand, but in 1960 the beach races were abandoned for a modern, banked circuit, where they still take place. As it is eight miles (13km) out of town, the races have become separated from Bike Week. They are more of a mainstream motorcycling event, dominated, like most competitions, by the four big Japanese manufacturers. Down on the beach, although there are more Japanese bikes than you would see at Sturgis, it is soon obvious which is the riders' favourite maker.

When the racing moved out of town

Big man, big bike: he is about to lay claim to the sole remaining parking spot left on Main Street, currently occupied by the photographer.

many regrets were voiced, but it has turned out to be a blessing for the whole event. It leaves the beach available for cruising. This has become the main activity of Bike Week. No helmet is required, and the open space and sea air make it much more pleasant than a city high street, although it has now become so popular that the would-be cruisers have to line up to take their turn. The pictures are misleading: the reason why they are taken looking out to sea is that no other direction offers a clear view. The beach is well policed too. Woe betide anyone speeding on the sand.

There is official drag racing on the beach and, as at Sturgis, many other attractions such as auto-jumbles, called swap meets in America, or just the sight of the bikes cruising slowly up and down Main Street. The Rat's Hole show is probably the most famous attraction. Held on the boardwalk on the Saturday, it is organized by Big Daddy Rat (Karl Smith) himself. There are numerous classes to suit the many different bikes on display. Choppers, low riders, vintage machines, dressers, street racers and, of course, rat bikes are present in hordes, and nearly all of them are Harleys. Being one of the best-known of custom shows, Rat's Hole embraces everything from backyard, home-brewed bikes to the latest creations of Arlen Ness and the other big custom houses. There are bikes produced for show and nothing else, others that are are purely dragsters, and more that are perfectly practical for everyday use. A welcome policy of the show is that everyone can come and, free of charge, wander among the bikes and gawp at the marvels as long as they like.

Earlier in the week, most of them will have been to the Harley-Davidson show at the Hilton. This is the occasion that leaves

no doubt of Harley's pre-eminent status at Daytona. The company takes over the Hilton's ballroom to display the latest V-twins. Its staff are there in force, and, with riders, dealers (current and retired) and company employees all meeting up to talk about bikes, it is as much a social event as a piece of corporate publicity.

The 1982 show was an especially important one for Harley. Not only was it the Sportster's 25th birthday, it was also the year of the Evolution engine. H-D's president, Charlie Thompson, and chief executive officer, Vaughn Beals, rode a pair of FLT Evos all the way from Washington State to prove their reliability. It was a successful stunt. Each bike used less than four ounces (1.4cl) of oil on the trip, and spent the rest of the week on show in the carpeted Hilton along with several other H-D staff bikes.

Outside the hotel, prospective buyers wanting test rides keep a fleet of demonstrators busy, while a ride-in show for Harley owners is held in the car park. Harley's top managers, often including Willie G. Davidson, make themselves generally available and, all in all, Daytona seems to be staging a Harley benefit. It's a PR man's dream: in Bike Week, the company can

RIGHT
Cruising Main Street is as important a part of the scene at Sturgis as at Daytona Beach, though you don't get the same wind-in-the-hair feeling.

seemingly do no wrong. Out near the race track is Harley Heaven, which is fundamentally a traditional bike rally with the usual games: slow races, bite the sausage competitions (an agile pillion passenger has to bite a chunk from a suspended frankfurter while moving underneath), and 'Just for Kicks' (how often can you kick-start your bike in one minute?).

This all helps to lure riders away from the crowded beach and the Rat's Hole and Hilton shows, and reduces the queue for the famous Boot Hill Saloon ('No Colors, Thankyou' says the sign outside), which normally stretches out onto the pavement. In spite of the huge numbers, and the potential conflict, Daytona is as trouble-free as Sturgis. There was a bad patch in the eighties, when some of the older residents objected to the fast-growing numbers of noisy bikes invading their peaceful seaside town, and the police responded with untoward zeal. It seems to have been a new police chief, Paul Crow, who restored general amity when he took over in 1988. It was as well that he did, not just for Harley and the thousands of Harley riders, but for Daytona itself. It may be less dependent on the bikers than Sturgis is, but it does pretty well all the same.

LEFT
A typical Main Street scene at Daytona. Although there is not a huge variety of different makes, you will find just about every conceivable type of Harley.

RIGHT
Variety is the spice of life at Daytona, witness this pink-clad grandmother with her matching dresser photographed outside the Hilton.

An all-chrome Sportster (with matching jacket) prepares for a blast. In fact, it would soon be stopped, as the police keep a close eye on beach traffic during Bike Week.

The ultimate dresser? This one has a total of 1,400 lights front and rear, or so the owner says (who else is going to count them?)

It was seen at the Rat's Hole show in 1978, where, as elsewhere at Daytona, the sheer variety of Harleys is one of the biggest attractions.

LEFT
Ride out from Daytona harbour. The red bike is Ken Denison's FXLR and the yellow is Tina Holtman's – both Razorback Harleys.

RIGHT
Tina Holtman's bike is one of the few complete machines built by Wyatt Fuller before his firm was taken over by Harley.

Chapter Seven
Image is All

Like it or not, Harley-Davidson depends on image, the image of the Harley owner as a free-wheeling, free-thinking, free spirit, somehow removed from the restrictions of job, mortgage or the need to get home in time to watch a favourite TV programme. He or she may in reality be nothing of the kind, but the bike still offers a chance to play that kind of part for a time, even if it's only on Sunday afternoons.

There's an image attached to any make of motorcycle, but it's stronger with Harley-Davidson than all others. Whatever practical reasons might be suggested for owning a Harley – good resale value, easy to work on, relaxed performance – the image is H-D's biggest asset in the marketplace. There are lots of V-twins around these days, and many that ape the Harley look, but none has quite the same appeal. Most are faster than a Harley, more convenenient and more refined (although the gap has been closing recently), but that slight suggestion of roughness is what some riders like about a Harley, that lack of compromise, the implied statement that 'what you see is what you get', and if you don't like it, too bad. In a world of constant compromise and ubiquitous regulation, it offers a sense of escape.

As we have seen, Harley-Davidson's image has changed quite dramatically over the years, and its changing history can be linked with the influence of the greatest modern image-maker, the cinema. Things began quite well. Apparently, the first Harley ever to appear on film was a JD that carried comedian Bill Dooley along in a silent slapstick comedy of 1926. In the thirties, when Harleys were the preferred mount of the police in many states, it became, on film, the enforcer of law and order, the equivalent of the white horse which, as every kid knew, was always ridden by the good guy. In the British film *No Limit*, motorbikes played a more neutral role, as both the hero and the villain rode in the TT, but of course there were no Harleys to be seen there. In the United States, since so many people could afford a car, bikes were ridden mainly by policemen and enthusiasts, and the latter included some film stars. A Harley is a popular 'fashion accessory' in Hollywood today, and that is not new: from the late thirties, to be photographed on a Harley was good publicity. Marlene Dietrich, Tyrone Power, Robert Taylor – all appeared in the H-D house magazine *The Enthusiast*. They may not have been able

110

to ride the machine, but some, Clark Gable for instance, were genuine enthusiasts.

The war also produced a good press for Harleys, with the famous WLAs playing a heroic front-line role in public information films. Things might have stayed that way indefinitely, but for *The Wild One*. Much has been written about Stanley Kubrick's 1953 film about small-town mayhem caused by a gang of marauding bikers. For the bike's public image, it was certainly a turning point. Instead of the hero on the white horse, Harley riders became the bad guys on horses of a very different colour, riding into town to bring trouble and violence to innocent citizens. In fact, Marlon Brando's Johnny is a good guy at heart, and the townspeople in the film are shown to be over-reacting, but such subtleties were lost on most of those who saw (or read about) the film. If it did not create it, the film did more to confirm the image of the bad biker than anything else, and, as Harley-Davidson dominated the market by this time, it followed that Harley riders were all ne'er-do-wells. Like officialdom's condemnation of the incident at Hollister, The *Wild One* confirmed the worst fears of parents while arousing the enthusiasm of their offspring in about equal proportion.

Whatever its effect on the image of motorcycling, the public loved the film and, inevitably, it spawned a whole succession of cheap and tatty imitations, designed to milk its newly identified audience. The biker films were chiefly notable for suspect acting, banal scripts and ridiculous plots, with the added ingredient of a gang of mean-looking Harley riders. Just as they seemed to have reached a dead end, something quite different came along. *Easy Rider* (1969) did not have much of a plot either, but it did portray two bikers facing a hostile world and suggested that, while motorcycling might well be outside the social mainstream, it offered a ticket to a kind of freedom.

ABOVE
In flamboyant rejection of wartime austerity, chrome covers areas it would never have touched in a WLA.

LEFT
Iain Cottrell's attention to detail has paid off: from this angle no one would guess the bike's humble origins.

RIGHT
A 1943 WLC owned by Mark Bently of Dorset, England. The British motorcycle industry suffered enormous damage from German air raids, and thousands of of WLs crossed the Atlantic to make good the loss.

LEFT
Harleys in the Badlands National Park, South
Dakota. One of the big attractions of Sturgis is
the superb riding country that surrounds it.

ABOVE
Ken Denison is even happier when sitting the
right way round. His yacht, Daybreak, is in the
background.

In a quite different and more acceptable way, *Easy Rider* was as important an influence as *The Wild One*. A year later it was backed up by the documentary-style *On Any Sunday*, which followed the fortunes of a Harley-Davidson factory rider, Mert Lawwill, through a racing season. It showed yet another aspect of motorcycling, this time as a sport, which the sensationalist films had ignored. At about the same time, the American TV show *Then Came Bronson* starred Michael Parks as the lone good guy zooming about on a Sportster.

Bike films since have been a mixed lot. Apart from the inevitable remakes with bikers as buffoons or hoodlums, there have been some notable high spots. *Electra Glide in Blue* (1973) remains the only film named after a motorcycle. Arnold Schwarzenegger, in his inimitable way, marshalled the big black Harley among the forces of righteousness in *The Terminator* (1984). *Mask* (1985), starring Cher and Sam Elliott, tells a moving story in which the best people happened to ride bikes. But perhaps the most convincing proof that the Hollywood image of Harley-Davidson has been rescued from the bad boys is its restoration as a publicity prop, with Schwarzenegger, Mickey Rourke and Sylvester Stallone among the well-known stars who have exploited it. It is said that if you want to stand out in Hollywood these days, the last thing you ride is a Harley. A dilapidated Honda moped would be more

ABOVE
A 1959 tank badge, still forward-looking and 'modern' in Harley's pre-nostalgia stage.

RIGHT
Set up for touring. In most Harleys, especially Sportsters and customs, the V-twin dominates everything else. In a full-dress Glide, it's the other way around.

likely to attract attention.

Macho actors like those mentioned above might be expected to ride a Harley. It's good for their image. They don't want to be seen as androgenous luvvies, all make-up and tantrums. They are regular guys, 'real' men in real life, and riding a Harley is a cheap and highly visible way of keeping up appearances. Perhaps they even enjoy riding their bikes.

There are other celebrity riders who don't fit that category, such as Crown Prince Olaf of Norway, the Earl of St Germans, and the late Malcolm Forbes. In spite of his giant Softail hot-air balloon, Forbes did not ride a motorcycle of any kind until quite late in life. But when he died at the age of 70, he left a cycle club, the Capitalist Tools, and a Harley at each of his houses, not to mention one on his private plane and two on the yacht. Peter de Savary, another millionaire businessman, known best for buying Land's End (the westernmost peninsula of England), was also a Harley man. He used to host HOG rallies on the lawns of his stately home.

In the very early days, the Harley was neither a glamorous fashion accessory nor a symbol of rebellious youth. To associate the motorcycle with social statements of that sort would have been wholly alien to Bill Harley and the three Davidson brothers. They were practical engineers, cautious, common-sense men, whose idea was not to make a glamorous object, or even a lot of money, but to produce a working motorcycle. The early Harleys were not great innovations, nor were they high performers, but they were reliable. Walter Davidson scored highest in the Long Island Endurance Run of 1908, and a week later the same bike won an economy

RIGHT

An attractive example of the W series in pale blue. This was more characteristic of the W's final years in production. Though relegated to a utility role, it had won a place in many hearts.

BELOW

This type of tank badge came between the elaborate, art deco style of the 1930s and the later attempts to recover the style of the early days. In the late 1940s, the name of Harley-Davidson had less nostalgic associations than it does now.

run at 188 miles per gallon. Such performances confirmed the early image of the Harley as a sound and sensible, economical machine. That reputation led to the official approval of Harleys by the U.S. Post Office for the RFD (Rural Free Delivery) service in 1915, and Harleys with sidecars remained the dominant postal-delivery vehicles throughout the 1920s.

Police contracts were equally valuable for public relations. The police were quick to move from horses to motorcycles: Pittsburgh bought a fleet of Harley-Davidson singles as early as 1909. They were essential to control the growing number of cars on the roads, as even the fastest horse could not keep up with a speeding Model T. As cars became faster, motorcycles had to follow suit, and a Harley or Indian V-Twin became the favourite mount of police patrols. Harley's ruthless business methods soon gave the company a virtual monopoly. In the mid-1920s about 3,000 police and civil service organizations were Harley-mounted. The police even took to the Servicar, which had been envisaged as a short-haul garage vehicle. It was not much use for chasing speedsters but proved ideal for the more leisurely business of enforcing parking regulations.

The Harley-Davidson was established as a reliable, no-nonsense machine, not the choice of speed freaks, and the new models produced right up to World War II reinforced that reputation. The equivalent Indian was almost invariably faster and flashier. Sporting riders might very well prefer an Indian or Excelsior, but the touring clubs, which were expanding rapidly, preferred the reliable Harley, whose first producers, still in charge, were now well into middle age and something like symbols of reliability themselves.

Then came the Knucklehead. Fast and stylish, if a little leaky, it leaped ahead of the opposition and gave the company a performance flagship. From then on, two disparate groups of H-D riders could be distinguished. The tourers had always been loyal and would remain so, but people who rode for the sheer thrill of speed were now also attracted to Harley. This was the type of rider who, after the war, would discard the heavy mudguards and screens in the quest for more speed.

The image was not changed so much as split. The speed merchants became customizers, associated (often without justification) with a dangerous, outlaw life style. Harleys were their usual choice (British bikes made inroads later but at first were seen as too cute and effete), which naturally affected the company image. Harley was the wild one, the rebel's machine. But it was also still the bike of the respectable tourers, who went on quietly cruising around the country on their full dressers. On the one hand were the Motor Maids of America, inoffensive as milkmaids in their smart uniforms. On the other hand, rough, tough and uncompromising, was the Boozefighters Motorcycle Club.

The latter element is markedly absent from H-D's advertising of the time. You would never know the Boozefighters existed. According to the ads, the 1952 Hydra-Glide gave its rider, 'youthful, invigorating, outdoor fun!... [It] brings you a host of new pals...a new world of outdoor sport, travel, adventure...' It sounded like some impossibly healthy hiking club for blandly virtuous young men and women. The latter, incidentally, were shown riding bikes, to emphasize the Harley's docility, and other aspects mentioned were economy, riding to work, and the sheer

practicality of a Harley-Davidson motorcycle. It was a touching reminder of H-D's original qualities, but it failed to recognize what had happened to the market since: people were no longer choosing to ride a motorcycle because they could not afford a car. Customizing, tuning and the biker lifestyle had all become part of the Harley world in the 1950s, but the company chose to ignore them. As a result, it antagonized many of its customers. It became a truism that Harley owners loved their bikes but hated the company that made them.

But, just as the Knucklehead had transformed Harley's image in 1936, the Super Glide did the same in 1970. Here at last was official recognition of what Harley owners had been doing to their machines for years. As far as Milwaukee was concerned, chopping was now fine, and it was that acceptance which laid the basis for the company's current success. Bikes like the Lowrider and Softail continued in the same vein: Harley had realized that the chopper crowd were good business.

Some friction remained, especially in the AMF days. AMF may have saved Harley-Davidson from financial collapse, but it wanted to stamp its own authority on every aspect of the business. When H-D booked a full-page ad in *Easyriders* (the outlaw monthly whose glossy cover was more famous for nude women than motorcycles), AMF was shocked. This would do its corporate image no good at all. It ordered H-D to withdraw the ad, and *Easyriders* responded by leaving the page blank save for a little box stating that Harley-Davidson regarded the magazine as bad for its image. As it was the largest-circulation monthly of its kind, the result was a public-relations disaster. It is easy to sympathize with the company. Harley was in a quandary: on one hand it did not want to uspset its hard-core loyalists, on the other it could not afford to put off potential buyers currently riding Japanese bikes.

A compromise was reached. AMF agreed that ads should be run in monthlies like *Easyriders* as long as its logo was removed and the ad was credited to the dealer network rather than Harley-Davidson itself. That involved some accounting manipulation, as the dealers were not actually paying for these national ads, but it did the trick for a time. The real significance of the incident was that it confirmed H-D's recognition of its loyalist riders, even if they did not conform to the conventional company image, long since discarded.

In the 1980s, after AMF had pulled out, Harley-Davidson began to embrace the biker life style (with emphasis on 'style') more enthusiastically. The Harley Owners Groups (HOG), launched in 1983, were a good example of the new approach. Every buyer of a new Harley automatically qualified for membership and could hang out at weekends with other members of the local chapter. HOG has been an astonishing success. There are now 600 chapters across the world with over 150,000 members. The whole operation is administered by a fourth-generation Bill Davidson, much better than some faceless corporate executive in a suit. HOG is a mixture of the old touring clubs, retaining an almost family atmosphere at some meetings and supporting charities like the Muscular Dystrophy Association, with hints of the biker life style – plenty of bandanas to be seen but no neckties. No other manufacturer has succeeded in selling membership of a way of life (even if only on Sundays) along with the bike. Mike Keefe, advertising manager in the 1980s, explained the company's policy quite frankly. 'We're starting to sell the entire Harley-Davidson experience. With the establishment of local HOG chapters, everything you need to enjoy the sport is at your H-D dealer. We offer the whole environment, something no other bike maker can match.'

Recently, Willie G. Davidson remarked that motorcyles had long ceased to be mere transportation. That was not universally popular, as it implied approval of wheeling the bike out on a sunny Sunday while using a car for getting about the rest of the week. In spite of its current success, Harley still needs to be careful. As ever, the company cannot afford to ignore the great band of loyal owners for whom their bike is part of everyday life. Fortunately, though, the attraction of the Harley is the same for everyone. It is encapsulated in slogans such as, 'Until you've been on a Harley-Davidson, you haven't been on a motorcycle', or 'More a way of life', or the ubiquitous T-shirt proclamation, 'If I had to explain, you wouldn't understand'. These are phrases that describe a love affair.

RIGHT
The hand gear change is standard, but the gear lever is a custom item. The colour is nice too!

The Sportster Accessory

I sure like those Springers
& a Low Rider has always been
my idea of a real motorcycle,

yet this 30th Anniversary Sportster
feels more like a quarter horse for
me with its vibrations instead of bucking:

but one morning I came out to the garage
to find horseshit on the floor & would say
this is quite an official Harley accessory

that research & design got just right
for us who want things rustic & natural –
it's the ideal XLH option

that I'm sure will be
an Eagle Iron catalog
addition with less of a stink to it but
just as much
of a pile.

Hidden Harleys: The Small Bikes

Harley-Davidson makes big V-twins, everyone knows that. But for many years it also sold small, single-cylinder bikes. These machines, not all made in Milwaukee, reflected the company's desire to catch its customers young. Then as now, people often stayed loyal to the make they started with and, as Harley's smallest twin was the 750cc 45, that put it at an obvious disadvantage. There were three generations of small Harleys, but none of them was a genuinely original Harley design. They were either heavily influenced by existing designs, bolt for bolt copies, or they were another manufacturer's bike with a Harley badge on the tank.

The A and B singles of 1926 were examples of the need to compete. They were brought out in response to Indian's Prince, a simple, 21ci (344cc) single first marketed the previous year. Harley-Davidson bought several examples of the Prince, along with British 350cc equivalents, stripped them all down and designed its own version. The result, called the Peashooter, came in side-valve and overhead-valve versions. Neither was trouble-free. The side-valver had a tendency to seize if cruising too long near its 50mph top speed, while the ohv's

exposed valve gear required frequent lubrication and adjustment to prevent premature wear. Still, the side-valve version was cheap ($210, including acetylene lights) and, if treated with respect, quite reliable. The 65mph ohv did very well in 21ci-class racing between the wars. The Peashooters lasted until 1935, joined for a time by a 30ci (492cc) single that was really half a 61ci V-twin.

The second generation of baby Harleys was born after World War II. It was really a pre-war DKW, the same model that BSA engineers turned into the much-loved Bantam. Harley's version was called the S-125 and used basically the same 125cc two-stroke engine with total-loss lubrication. The Milwaukee version, producing just three horsepower and combined with rubber-band front suspension and a rigid rear end, made a thoroughly basic learner's bike. About 10,000 were sold in the first year, 1947, inheriting the market of the original Paperboy side-valves, but in spite of a few updates, such as Teleglide forks in 1951, and a couple of capacity increases, sales fell off. The Topper scooter (1960-65) suffered a similar fate. Like the BSA/Triumph equivalents, it was a belated - and unsuccessful - attempt to cash in on the success of the trendy Italian scooters.

Harley-Davidson's response was to buy 50 per cent of Aermacchi, an Italian maker of small, four-stroke singles that was in financial trouble. This provided the opportunity to sell a modern 250 at a competitive price, and Aermacchis were soon crossing the Atlantic badged as Harley-Davidson Sprints. The inevitable problems included quality control on the electrics, not to mention communication difficulties between the Italian and U.S.

ABOVE
An early Aermacchi. This represented Harley's hope of getting back into the small-bike market and, for a time, it worked, whatever some of the less progressive dealers may have thought.

Attempts to update the Sprint were limited to colour changes and downtubes for the frame, which made the bike look bigger than it really was.

ABOVE
There was nothing revolutionary about the four-stroke Aermacchi single, and it fitted comfortably into the Harley-Davidson tradition.

factories. In spite of the problems, the Sprint did relatively well. By the standards of the sixties it was fast and lightweight, probably a better bike than the British equivalents in the 250 class. Sales reflected that, averaging 5,000 a year in the late sixties and peaking at 9,000 in 1967, when it outsold the Sportster, although some Harley dealers treated these small machines with considerable disdain.

Against Japanese competition, however, the Sprint soon began to look outdated. To meet the Japanese challenge a whole range of Aermacchi two-strokes was produced, including a moped, the 100cc Enduro, and a series of 125-250cc trail bikes. Notwithstanding modern accoutrements, such as trail-bike styling, five-speed gearbox and oil injection, these all succumbed eventually, though they sold quite well for a time. They were finally dropped in 1977, when Harley-Davidson reverted to producing what it does best – big V-twins.

The young lady is modelling the latest in Federal- and European Community-approved anti-abrasion gear. Or is this bondage by motorcycle?

LEFT
The helmet slogan says it all. Plenty of women ride their own Harleys and enjoy their independence.

ABOVE
'Down at the dealers' means something different at Sturgis. According to rumour, this dealer is closed for 51 weeks of the year.

Rushmore Office Supplies finds less demand for notepads and rulers during Bike Week, so they sell ice creams instead.

Index